C000212498

3 Kafka: Die Verwandlung

Critical Guides to German Texts

EDITED BY MARTIN SWALES

KAFKA

Die Verwandlung

John Hibberd

Senior Lecturer in German
University of Bristol

Grant & Cutler Ltd
2000

© Grant & Cutler Ltd 2000

ISBN 0 7293 0422 1

First edition 1985
Reprinted, with supplementary bibliography, 2000

DEPÓSITO LEGAL: V. 312 - 2000

Printed in Spain by
Artes Gráficas Soler, S.A., Valencia
for
GRANT & CUTLER LTD
55-57 GREAT MARLBOROUGH STREET, LONDON, W1V 2AY

Contents

Author's Note

The page numbers in brackets in my text refer to pages of *Die Verwandlung* in the 1981 reprint of the widely available 1977 paperback edition of *Das Urteil und andere Erzählungen* (Fischer Taschenbuch Verlag). Other volumes of Kafka's works are indicated by the following abbreviations:

B. — *Beschreibung eines Kampfes* (S. Fischer Verlag, 1954)

Br. — *Briefe 1902-1924* (S. Fischer Verlag, 1958)

BrF. — *Briefe an Felice und andere Korrespondenz aus der Verlobungszeit* (S. Fischer Verlag, 1967)

H. — *Hochzeitsvorbereitungen auf dem Lande und andere Prosa aus dem Nachlaß* (Fischer Taschenbuch Verlag, 1980)

In the footnotes an italicised figure refers to the numbered entry in my Select Bibliography.

Introduction

In the preface to his Spanish translation of *Die Verwandlung* the Argentinian, Jorge Luis Borges, himself an outstanding figure in twentieth-century world literature, observed that it is the most memorable of Kafka's stories and one of the most important works of this century. Borges' assessment, made in 1938,[1] is not unique and it needs no revision now. With its unforgettable opening, its telling images of isolation, frustration and rejection, its flavour of a personal nightmare with a wider symbolic meaning, *Die Verwandlung* has a truly exceptional power to haunt the imagination and the memory. It has played a large part in determining the general image of its author and in influencing the use of the adjective 'Kafkaesque' to denote, not so much the unique world of his fiction, but rather any experience that is extraordinary and frightening and puzzling and very real despite its apparent incredibility. Kafka is, indeed, for many synonymous with the young man who wakes up to discover that his body has been transformed into that of an insect; for *Die Verwandlung* is the most widely read of his stories. Kafka wrote other masterpieces, other stories which are equally fantastic and strange, gripping and depressing; at least one (*In der Strafkolonie*) which is more horrible; others, too, which are less harrowing and where the playfulness of his imagination, his humour and irony are more immediately striking. Some of his works are more ambitious in scope. But none is more memorable or effective than *Die Verwandlung*.

Without its power to grip and move, this story would not have the historical importance recognised by Borges. It would not have so impressed another Latin-American writer, the Colombian Gabriel García Márquez, that it moved him at the age of nineteen to read 'all' the novels of world literature (the

[1] Reprinted in J.L. Borges, *Prólogos* (Buenos Aires, Torres Agüero, 1975), p.103.

'all' need not, in the context of South American rhetoric, be taken too literally). García Márquez was particularly struck by the importance of fantasy as the starting point of *Die Verwandlung*.[2] He was probably unaware that fantasy was characteristic of much earlier German writing, particularly in the Romantic period, and that Kafka was influenced by the tales of E.T.A. Hoffmann which entertained and bemused generations of nineteenth-century readers. But Kafka's fantasy is distinctly modern in that it is anchored in the contemporary world, and refuses ultimately to offer an attractively superior vantage-point from which to view reality. By recording an event which flouts all familiar expectations of causality, Kafka indeed took a significant step, significant, because of its success, in the beginnings of 'progressive' twentieth-century fiction which in one way or another rejects the conventions and aims of literary realism.

This break with realism — and it is almost synonymous with Kafka's 'modernity' and his historical importance — has several dimensions. One is the restriction of the perspective (for most of the text) in a third-person narrative to that of the main character. Kafka's hero is imprisoned in his subjective world. The themes of the individual's isolation and of the impossibility of communication, so characteristic of modern fiction, are connected with the inaccessibility of an objectively or generally recognised and valid truth. Kafka's refusal to provide a reliable basis for understanding and judging characters and events is basic to his depiction of a world that withholds ultimate meaning. Sartre, Camus, and the 'new novelists' of France admired his work as an authentic rendering of subjective experience which they saw as the only true mode of experience. Indeed many writers and thinkers attempting to describe or analyse the condition of modern man have been persuaded, but for many different reasons, that Kafka depicted that condition with great insight and power. W.H. Auden spoke for many when he said: 'Had one to name the author who comes nearest to bearing the same kind of relation to our age as Dante,

[2] G. García Márquez, *El olor de la guayaba: conversaciones con P.A. Mendoza* (Barcelona, Bruguera, 1982), pp.41ff., 70.

Shakespeare and Goethe bore to theirs, Kafka is the first name one would think of.'[3]

Such a claim to great representative stature for Kafka may seem to fit oddly with the clearly very personal quality of his writing and the restrictedness of its scope. Some critics, indeed, maintain that he portrays only the sickness of his own mind and was blind to the real problems of the world. The disagreement about Kafka's status has been most bitter in the Marxist world (though by no means confined to it, for adherents to other philosophies and religions have held contradictory views of his work). In Eastern Europe this controversy assumes political significance because literary realism is part of established party dogma.[4] Not every reader of *Die Verwandlung* will be inclined to take the issue of realism quite so seriously. Nevertheless he will surely ask: 'How does this strange tale relate to reality, my reality, and to what part of it?' Doubts about the utter seriousness with which most commentators approach *Die Verwandlung* are apposite to that question. The story is compelling and distressing, even tragic. But it is also puzzling, and a part of the puzzle is ignored if we do not recognise distinct signs of irony in the narrative. The earnestness of the thoughts reported and the depth of feeling expressed stand at odds with the absurdity of the patently unreal situations. (Those critics who say that Kafka makes us believe in the metamorphosis of his hero as if it were real are, of course, half right. But we can never entirely forget that this is fiction, and fantastic fiction at that.) That discrepancy between seriousness and absurdity is basically comic, though the humour is black. Here we have farcical exaggeration and tragedy, indistinguishable one from another. No single emotional or intellectual response on the part of the fictional characters or of the reader seems quite appropriate. That is ultimately the most disturbing feature of this tale, and a characteristic of 'modernist' writing. Normal reactions seem out of place, yet there is nothing to serve in their stead as a guide to

[3] W.H. Auden, 'The Wandering Jew', *New Republic*, 10 February 1941, reprinted in D. Jakob, *Das Kafka-Bild in England*, Vol.2 (Oxford and Erlangen, D. Jakob, 1971), p.409.

[4] See K. Hughes, 'The Marxist Debate' in *16*, pp.51ff.

understanding, acting and judging.

Kafka himself would scarcely have been surprised by all the critical argument about *Die Verwandlung*, nor by the embarrassment it was capable of causing. But its success and fame he apparently did not expect, even though it was one of the very few stories by him that he considered worthy of publication. Typically he abandoned most of the works he started, for he had high standards and despaired of his own ability. The bulk of his oeuvre, including the unfinished novels *Der Prozeß* and *Das Schloß* which did so much to establish his reputation, was published after his death in 1924 by his friend, Max Brod, who ignored Kafka's instruction to burn his manuscripts. But *Die Verwandlung* had already occasioned some admiration since its first appearance in 1916. It was written in 1912, a year which marked, as Kafka sensed at the time, his breakthrough as a writer. He was then twenty-nine years old. Fellow writers among his friends (Brod foremost among them) had already made a name for themselves. Yet only now was his first book (*Betrachtung*) about to appear, a small collection of prose pieces written in earlier years which fell short of what he hoped to achieve. Nevertheless, impending publication of this volume was some encouragement. Moreover, in September 1912 he wrote his first great short story, *Das Urteil*. He had always felt compelled to write, he had been writing for years, but now his doubts about his ability receded, temporarily. There remained great worries about being distracted, interrupted and discouraged by his family. He lived with his parents, and his involvement in his brother-in-law's business venture, added to his work in an insurance company, left him little free time. He wrote mostly in the still of the night. *Das Urteil*, composed at one sitting in the course of a single night, is the only work with which we know he was unambiguously pleased, largely because it was written so quickly and without interruption. In the next days he began the second version of the novel *Amerika* (he had destroyed his first draft earlier that year). By mid-November he had completed six chapters, but then he set the novel aside and started *Die Verwandlung*. After struggling with the later stages of the story, and after the unwelcome break of a business trip, he finished it three weeks later. Increasingly he regretted interrupting work on *Amerika* which was never to be completed. *Die Verwandlung*, Kafka wrote while working on it, was exceptionally disgusting (BrF., p.117). A diary entry of 19 January 1914 shows that by then his dissatisfaction had grown to an intense dislike:

> Großer Widerwille vor 'Verwandlung'. Unlesbares Ende.
> Unvollkommen fast bis in den Grund.

There were personal reasons for this aversion to which I wish to return later.

In *Das Urteil* nothing absolutely inconceivable happens, though the motivation of its characters is obscure and in the course of the story their reactions become incredible. In *Die Verwandlung* the impossible event is central. It was *Das Urteil*, rather than *Die Verwandlung*, that Kafka regarded as the important confirmation of his vocation and promise of future development. But both stories served to strengthen his belief that his urge to write and the content of his writing were evidence of his unfitness for normal healthy life. In both he expressed his fear of his own unworthiness and weakness of character. Both tell of a son who accepts his condemnation by his father as an inescapable death sentence and proof of his inability to cope with the ordinary business of living. The same theme of parental rejection is found in *Amerika*, whose first chapter Kafka published as *Der Heizer*. He thought of having *Das Urteil*, *Die Verwandlung* and *Der Heizer* published together under the title *Die Söhne*. They provide abundant material for comment on Kafka's strained relations with his father. In the *Brief an den Vater* written in 1919 Kafka himself depicted his whole life and all his writing as aspects of his struggle with his father. With its symptomatic mixture of self-justification and self-accusation, that letter (which was never delivered) is an important psychological and literary document. It tells us a great deal about the way in which Kafka's creative imagination fed on — and transcended — his particular psychological turmoil.

But Kafka planned another grouping of stories: *Das Urteil*, *Die Verwandlung* and *In der Strafkolonie* could make a volume

entitled *Strafen*. By 1914, when he wrote *In der Strafkolonie* and
Der Prozeß, the theme of parental authority had been widened
to that of an incomprehensible judicial system which appears to
have the divine attribute of omnipotence but not that of mercy,
and whose justice is highly questionable. *Das Urteil* and *Die
Verwandlung* also, in embryonic form, suggest the theme of *Das
Schloß*, written in 1922: the outsider battling for acceptance and
recognition in a society ruled by a power and by principles that
he cannot satisfy, understand or accept. For both *Der Prozeß*
and *Das Schloß* develop themes which we find in the earlier
stories: the isolation of the bachelor hero, his hopeless struggle
with the world, the impossibility of communication and comprehension. *Die Verwandlung* heralds another development in
Kafka's fiction: his use of animal figures in pieces which ask
what is truly human or proper in man — the desire to conform,
to find security in the herd, to copy others and find their
approval and material success, or the need for absolute freedom
and truth, to reject the common mean and to pursue spiritual
goals even though they may prove unobtainable. In later stories
Kafka was much concerned with the claims of the writer or artist
to public acclaim. He was not the only writer of this century to
inherit from Romanticism (and to magnify) worries about the
pathology of the creative artist. He was worried about the justification and function of fiction because he was not sure of the
reality or truth it aimed to depict or discover. What is true and
real and right? *Die Verwandlung* is itself concerned with such
questions within what at first seems a narrow framework of
reference. But when related to its biographical background and
to his other works, including his letters and diaries, and indeed
to the broader intellectual context of the age in which he lived,
the potentially endless ramifications of its doubts become more
evident and more suggestive. Writers have always sought new
ways to portray reality but only in this century have they
commonly been uncertain of what is real, and none has been
more desperately uncertain than Kafka.

Kafka presents and explores situations and problems in
images, by analogy and imaginative exaggeration; by a curiously
logical pursuit of relations between the concrete and the

abstract, mental events and the external world. He takes metaphor literally and uses it to move from a picture of a condition to the generation of a story. For the world of inner experience he portrays cannot be expressed in concrete terms except by analogy. The 'poetic' manner of thinking was natural to him and it marks all his writing — novels, stories, sketches and fragments, aphorisms, diary entries and letters. But nowhere is his exploration of metaphor more obvious and more striking than in *Die Verwandlung*. For that reason this story may be seen as quintessential Kafka fiction and has been a central point in critics' investigations into his literary technique and significance.

Always Kafka was concerned with himself and his own hopelessly conflicting emotions and ideas. Yet he supposed that his own condition, so obviously exceptional, nevertheless mirrored, even if in a distorted and exaggerated form, the condition of many, perhaps even all. Among the many, he included first and foremost other writers who struggled with their vocation and suffered in their experience of men and the world; and fellow Jews who had been separated from their faith and their roots. He also thought of his contemporaries in general, all those who could not identify with a community or a philosophical conviction and did not feel at ease in the world, those for whom life was an unending search for belief in its meaningfulness. This concern with general or even universal significance is felt in *Die Verwandlung* in its hints of psychological, sociological or religious meaning, even if such claims to profundity are presented as teasers rather than with the ring of solemn truth.

Great art often arises from suffering. Kafka's writing certainly did, but it was motivated by only the frailest hope that it might bring him release through understanding. His suffering had several causes: his relations with his parents and the women he loved; his position as a Jew without religious faith within a society where anti-semitic attitudes were common and anti-semitic violence not unknown; as a German-speaker in a country whose Czech-speaking majority resented, along with Austrian rule in general, the dominance of German-speakers in their capital, his city of Prague. Not least there was the general breakdown of traditional beliefs, more particularly of faith even in man's capacity to explain himself and the world, which both undermined the writer's hopes of justifying his writing and made the task of social assimilation and integration into the immediate community of his family more pressing and more difficult. But Kafka's greatest misfortune, and a source of his genius, was his extraordinary emotional and moral sensitivity and his ability to see complexities, both real and imagined, in every situation. His awareness of conflicting demands, and of conflicting interpretations (possibly equally valid and thus equally dubious) of almost every matter, including his own motives, meant that he was always subject to terrible indecision and insecurity. He bore his inner conflicts with resigned humour and fortitude though he came to believe that they were destroying him. When the tuberculosis from which he was to die was diagnosed in 1917 he saw this disease as the physical manifestation of mental and emotional battles within him. Because these battles had been fought most energetically in his writing, he himself dated, quite unscientifically, the first sign of his fatal illness to the night he wrote *Das Urteil*.

Fear, disgust, and wonder are the stuff of *Die Verwandlung*. We may subsequently discover that this story mirrors various preoccupations more generally characteristic of recent times. But we cannot fail to recognise the skill with which it is told, and to sense immediately that, for all its grotesque fantasticality, Kafka here throws a remarkably revealing light on questions of family relationships and of self-appraisal which matter to everyone.

1. A Structure and a Strategy

The opening of *Die Verwandlung* is certainly striking and memorable: two worlds — that of normal reality and that of irrationality — collide:

> Als Gregor Samsa eines Morgens aus unruhigen Träumen erwachte, fand er sich in seinem Bett zu einem ungeheueren Ungeziefer verwandelt. Er lag auf seinem panzerartig harten Rücken und sah, wenn er den Kopf ein wenig hob, seinen gewölbten, braunen, von bogen-förmigen Versteifungen geteilten Bauch, auf dessen Höhe die Bettdecke, zum gänzlichen Niedergleiten bereit, kaum noch erhalten konnte. Seine vielen, im Vergleich zu seinem sonstigen Umfang kläglich dünnen Beine flimmerten ihm hilflos vor den Augen.
> 'Was ist mit mir geschehen?' dachte er. Es war kein Traum. (p.19)

The nightmarish horror of the situation is graphically captured, not least by the registering of the disconnection between mind and limbs. Gregor's question and the denial that he is dreaming can hardly fail to incite the reader to ask further questions. Why has this metamorphosis taken place, why is he, the reader, called to believe the impossible, what sense can it all make? Of course the question 'what will happen next?' is paramount, and it is this that makes us read on. The beginning of the story has an over-riding importance both as a puzzle to be solved and as a pre-condition of subsequent events. From it the narrative develops with a clear sense of direction towards the end. That end we expect to bring a solution to the questions 'how?' and 'why?' which naturally complement the hero's question 'what has happened?' The division of the story into three parts based on a principle of parallel and contrast suggests a clarity of structure

which by its very presence as creation of order promises meaning
and therefore an answer to the mystery.

Already in the first part there is movement towards a decisive
climax compared with which the opening, however striking, is
relatively low-key. The matter-of-fact tone which gives the
initial sentences their force will not be sustained. Gregor himself
is far from being as disturbed and excited by his metamorphosis
as he is by later events. His apparent lack of surprise adds to the
shock experienced by the reader who senses that Gregor is
poorly prepared for what may come and is intrigued by the
hero's reaction. For Gregor allows his thoughts to wander away
from the metamorphosis itself. Time passes and little happens
until — forty minutes and over six pages later — the chief clerk
or office manager arrives to investigate Gregor's absence from
work. At that moment, with a shock of consternation (though
he expects such a visit), Gregor falls from his bed. Matters now
come to a head. The pace quickens. With difficulty he unlocks
his door and emerges from his room. His appearance in the
doorway, his entry into the living-room and the reaction of
parents and chief clerk together form a series of climaxes. Now
horror is registered in the text itself, though by those who see
Gregor rather than by the hero himself. The drama continues
until the first section ends as he is driven back into his room by
his father.

Whereas one sentence established the fact of the metamorphosis, a paragraph is needed to recount Gregor's efforts to
open his door. The emotional tone rises. The reactions of
parents and chief clerk are described in vivid detail. But for the
context they would be exaggeratedly histrionic. The time for
attempts to remain calm and collected has passed, and with it the
leisurely pace of the narrative as Gregor lay musing or made
slow and deliberate efforts to get out of bed. Now the shriek and
the gestures of the chief clerk set the tone; the language of the
narrative is controlled and aims at precision, but it is not the
precision of sobriety:

> da hörte [Gregor] schon den Prokuristen ein lautes 'Oh!'
> ausstoßen — es klang, wie wenn der Wind saust — und

nun sah er ihn auch, wie er, der der Nächste an der Türe war, die Hand gegen den offenen Mund drückte und langsam zurückwich, als vertreibe ihn eine unsichtbare, gleichmäßig fortwirkende Kraft. (p.31)

der Prokurist war schon auf der Treppe; das Kinn auf dem Geländer, sah er noch zum letzten Male zurück. Gregor nahm einen Anlauf, um ihn möglichst sicher einzuholen; der Prokurist mußte etwas ahnen, denn er machte einen Sprung über mehrere Stufen und verschwand: 'Hu!' aber schrie er noch, es klang durchs ganze Treppenhaus. (p.34)

Excitement is conveyed in sentences where semicolons separate several main clauses. The same rhythm of excitement, intensified by the non-repetition of the subject pronouns, is found in the paragraph (pp.33-34) which leads up to the mother's horrified reaction:

Und ohne daran zu denken, daß er seine gegenwärtigen Fähigkeiten, sich zu bewegen, noch gar nicht kannte, ohne auch daran zu denken, daß seine Rede möglicher- ja wahrscheinlicherweise wieder nicht verstanden worden war, verließ er den Türflügel; schob sich durch die Öffnung; wollte zum Prokuristen hingehen, der sich schon am Geländer des Vorplatzes lächerlicherweise mit beiden Händen festhielt; fiel aber sofort, nach Halt suchend, mit einem kleinen Schrei auf seine vielen Beinchen nieder. (p.33)

Unthinking, instinctive movements characterise this climax. Now, rather than when the metamorphosis itself is registered by Gregor, it becomes explicit that the characters are apparently subject to powers beyond their control, perhaps even to a supernatural force ('eine unsichtbare ... Kraft' (p.31)) and what happens cannot be adequately described or explained. Immediately before, at the moment when Gregor appears at the door, but before he moves into the living-room, the motion is held in suspense while the scene in the room is described (p.31)

and Gregor's speech is related (p.32). But once the climax has
been reached the pitch of excitement is maintained over three
pages of text. As Gregor retreats before his father the same rush
of clauses linked by a minimum of co-ordinating conjunctions is
again noticeable:

> Vielmehr trieb er [der Vater], als gäbe es kein Hindernis,
> Gregor jetzt unter besonderem Lärm vorwärts; es klang
> schon hinter Gregor gar nicht mehr wie die Stimme bloß
> eines einzigen Vaters; nun gab es wirklich keinen Spaß
> mehr, und Gregor drängte sich — geschehe was wolle — in
> die Tür. Die eine Seite seines Körpers hob sich, er lag schief
> in der Türöffnung, seine eine Flanke war ganz
> wundgerieben, an der weißen Tür blieben häßliche Flecken
> ... (p.36)

After all this commotion — the disarray of the characters is
paralleled by the whirlwind draught in the living-room (p.35) —
and after a detailed and highly wrought account, the final clause
of the first section — 'dann wurde es endlich still' — is as
effective as the matter-of-fact opening of the story. It has a ring
of finality, though clearly the tale of Gregor has not finished yet.
The first part has been brought to its close. *Die Verwandlung*
begins with an unforgettable picture of Gregor waking to discover his metamorphosis. And later in its first section
memorable images abound: Gregor turning the key of his door
by moving his whole body round the key in his mouth; the chief
clerk's flight; the mother standing with outstretched arms and
splayed fingers and collapsing on to the table; the father with
clenched fist and sobbing breast; Gregor shooed back by his
father wielding a stick and a newspaper or stuck in the door
before he is pushed back into his room. Gregor's initial
ponderings have given way to decisive action. Gregor indeed
intends that the results of his emergence from his room should
determine whether he can be expected to continue a normal life.
As his intention is reported, the craziness of his resolve to appear
before the others is indicated by the repeated 'tatsächlich':

Er wollte tatsächlich die Tür aufmachen, tatsächlich sich sehen lassen und mit dem Prokuristen sprechen (p.28)

Given his appearance and his inability to communicate, the response to his appearance is not unexpected. Already in this first phase of the story we feel shocked but not too surprised; a sense of inevitability is being established; we recognise that the narrative has been carefully organised and scrupulously paced.

The two further sections also begin rather quietly and then move to a climax when Gregor again enters the living-room. These climaxes too are marked by a series of main clauses, often with the subject omitted, separated by semicolons. The second section like the first begins with Gregor's awakening and ends as he is driven back into his room by his father. In the third part he returns to his room of his own accord. The story concludes with a description of events after his death in four pages (pp.69-73) which are best considered as an epilogue. The threefold repetition of Gregor's attempt to make contact with others underlines the sense of inevitability. If there was little hope in the beginning of Gregor's being understood and accepted, there is even less later. Kafka's difficulty with the later stages of his story cannot have arisen because he did not know how it would finish. Unless Gregor's metamorphosis is reversed his relations with his family are bound to deteriorate. He is not even fit to be an interesting pet. If he has any feelings for his family at all he must, like his sister and father, conclude that everyone will be happier without him. Signs of hope or consolation in the middle section — Gregor learns to control his new body, the family may after all manage to support themselves, his sister takes pride in caring for him, his mother clings to hopes of his recovery — prove deceptive, and that only adds to the impression that deterioration is inevitable.

There is a progressive decline in Gregor's physical condition. In section one he discovers that his body will respond to his wishes (but does not note that his mobility makes him terrifying to others). In section two the injuries sustained when he was thrust through the door heal remarkably quickly. The fall from his bed was painful; now he drops nonchalantly from the ceiling.

But his sight worsens and he loses his appetite. In section three
there is no recovery from the wound in his back inflicted by his
father during his second venture into the living-room. He eats
nothing and does not sleep. He now crawls slowly over the floor;
already before the third climax he is 'zum Sterben müde und
traurig' (p.61). For Gregor's spiritual decline is equally
apparent. At first he desperately wants to help his family and
spares no effort to persuade the chief clerk of his willingness to
work. In the second section he is more passive, intent on
showing consideration towards his family (p.38) and grateful for
their ministrations. His risky appearance before his mother,
dictated by the hope of maintaining contact with his human
past, is meant to be 'möglichst rücksichtsvoll' (p.50). In the last
phase he resents the family's neglect of him and all thoughts of
considerateness are forgotten (p.63).

As Gregor's condition and attitude change, so do those of his
relatives. Here there are progressions that are set in counterpoint
to his development, though that they may from one point of
view be changes for the better does not become manifest until
the epilogue. They are, however, marked, and they are as surprising as the initial metamorphosis of Gregor. In the second
section Gregor is struck by a complete transformation in his
father ('war das noch der Vater?' (p.53)). In the third part the
sister on whom many of his hopes were pinned, the girl who was
still a child, becomes the hardheaded realist who rejects his
claims on the family and their responsibility for him. Her change
from helpless concern to dutiful caring and then to resentment is
the most significant development in the story. It is connected
with some complex patterns of interrelation between the
characters which will be investigated in a later chapter. But some
changes and suggestions of connections may be noted now: as
Gregor's strength of purpose fades, so in those around him
panic gives way to stoicism, hostility and decisiveness. In part
one the chief clerk flees; in part two the mother faints; in part
three no one faints or flees. The family has grown more used to
the horror. In the last section the charwoman and the lodgers are
emotionally immune to Gregor. The first servant (the cook)
quits her job; the second remains immured in the kitchen, well

away from Gregor, until she is dismissed; the third, the char-woman, threatens him with a chair. This sequence too parallels the hardening of attitudes in the family. The 'es' of the sister's dreadful conclusion, 'wir müssen versuchen, es loszuwerden' (p.66), in which Gregor is finally declared to be non-human, is echoed in the charwoman's proclamation, 'es ist krepiert' (p.69), and in her satisfied announcement that no one need worry any longer about 'das Zeug von nebenan' (p.72). Gregor, who habitually locks himself in his room at night, is sub-sequently locked in by his family; later the door is left open, as another sign that their fear has diminished. At the beginning Gregor frightens the chief clerk; towards the end he fails to scare the charwoman. His father drives the three lodgers from the flat, and does so deliberately, whereas Gregor drove away the chief clerk when he wanted him to stay. The family's economic situation worsens with Gregor's condition. They have to dispense with servants and make do with a daily help, to sell some possessions, find jobs and to take in lodgers. Signs of increasing confidence and capability in father and sister are largely offset by their evident weariness, but the importance of their new strength becomes evident in the last pages.

The three sections of the story are like acts in a drama. There are effective 'curtains' after each climax. The concentration on gesture, significant visual details and groupings of characters, and the relative lack of dialogue suggest, however, an even closer likeness to the early silent films that Kafka knew well. It is not unhelpful to think of each sequence in terms of camera and editing technique, of long shots and close-ups, movement from one figure or object to another, a prolonged still. These analogies with theatre or film immediately suggest emotional intensity. Kafka's story indeed strikes the reader as dictated by strong emotion. But the same analogies also suggest studied timing, deliberate build-up of tension, conscious striving for effect and conscious exaggeration.

The patterns in *Die Verwandlung* so far observed establish dramatic climaxes, underline the inevitability of the hero's decline into death, and the contrast between that decline and the fate of his relatives. They constitute a structure that is

aesthetically effective and pleasing. The story is, indeed, master-
fully constructed. As a good story should, it begins with a puzzle
or intriguing promise and proceeds to unfold connections. But
here the connections I have noted fall short of the anticipated
meaning. They do not explain Gregor's metamorphosis. They
do not suggest a cause and a possible remedy for the regrettable
condition that is the object of analysis. Conflict, latent at the
beginning, is intensified until at the end tension is released as
normality reasserts itself. Gregor is freed in death from suffering
and his family finds hope for the future. The parallel with the
structure of a tragedy is, however, only partial. The hero's guilt
has not been clearly established. It is not clear that he is
responsible for the metamorphosis and the mode of existence
that are his crime. Rather he seems a victim of an inexplicable
random event. The formal coherence of the story does not serve
to clarify the initial puzzle. Despite its evident artistic control
Die Verwandlung seems in a sense incomplete and designed to
frustrate ultimate understanding. Another aspect of this incompleteness is to be noted in the description of the insect itself.

  The first partial description of the insect conveys the horror of
the sight. The details of Gregor's new shape that are then
revealed gradually as the narrative progresses do not altogether
surprise, for the calamitous nature of his dreadful change is
clear from the beginning. Yet each detail is striking and renews
the initial shock. We learn that Gregor has many thin legs and
that his feet are tactile. His back consists of hard plates; perhaps
they are linked by flexible membranes, for his body proves more
malleable than he at first supposes; perhaps, too, it is such a
membrane that is pierced by the apple thrown by his father — or
are the plates not so hard after all? His lower parts, invisible to
him, are rather sensitive and presumably softer. His jaws or
mandibles are strong but contain no teeth. He is brown in
colour, perhaps even his blood (or is it saliva?) is brown. He has
antennae, and maybe they function as organs of smell for they
lead him to food in the dark. He leaves trails of slime behind
him. Clearly he is repulsive to behold, most particularly because
his size is monstrous too. Compared with his former, human
proportions, his shape has changed considerably. His limbs are

small but his body has not shrunk to the size of an insect. His trunk has become broader, and perhaps a little shorter, for he reaches the key in the door with some difficulty when standing on his hind legs and needs to stand on a chair to look through the window. Upright he passes sideways through the door, but on all his feet he is too wide for it. No wonder then that his mother faints when she sees this man-sized creature spread-eagled on the flowered wallpaper. His obnoxiousness is further indicated by his taste in food (he appreciates only that which is fit for the dustbin) and by a hint that he impregnates his room with a vile smell — long before he is surrounded by filth his sister rushes to open the window as soon as she enters.

There is no doubt about the reactions Gregor provokes. But can we form a distinct image of him? Can we give a name, even, to this frightful creature? The charwoman calls him a 'Mistkäfer' (p.59); but here she expresses her disapproval and contempt; she does not identify him as a particular scientific species. The term used by the narrator in the first sentence is no more precise. An 'Ungeziefer' is a pest of small dimensions, likely to be parasitic and to carry infection and best exterminated, perhaps an object of morbid fascination: a louse, bug, flea or mosquito. The word may be applied to a human being who is a useless or parasitic nuisance. Kafka has taken the almost dead metaphor literally and given it new life. Since Gregor has many legs and his body is not said to be divided into thorax and abdomen, he is probably no true insect. He may look more like a louse or centipede.

The details of the description of Gregor are effective. Individually they smack of familiarity with the insect or anthropoid world. When Kafka says that Gregor's whole body moves with his mouth in the act of eating, that this creature bangs its head on the ground as it drags itself exhausted over the floor, and that its corpse is dry and shrivelled, that all seems convincingly authentic. But the question 'what sort of horrid insect is he?' is inappropriate and unanswerable. Significantly Kafka was appalled by the thought that the illustrator of his story might depict the 'Ungeziefer':

Nun habe ich einen ... Schrecken bekommen. Es ist mir
nämlich ... eingefallen, er könnte etwa das Insekt selbst
zeichnen wollen. Das nicht, bitte das nicht ... Das Insekt
selbst kann nicht gezeichnet werden. Es kann nicht einmal
von der Ferne aus gezeigt werden ... (Br., p.135f)

If we try to gather the details of Gregor's appearance into a
clear, coherent picture we discover that the description is
incomplete; in trying to equate his appearance with that of a real
creature we have proceeded against the spirit of the narrator's
technique. He does not give, in one passage, that full description
of his character that is so often found within the tradition of
realist writing which claims to give an objective and rounded
picture of reality.

The incompleteness of the piecemeal description of the
'Ungeziefer' may be explained simply as a means of allowing the
reader's imagination the room for manoeuvre so necessary when
a visual horror is to be evoked. But the same technique of
scattered delineation is used in the description of Gregor's room
and the family flat. Here there is little reason to leave much to
the reader's imagination, for the physical setting of the story is
by no means fantastic. On the contrary, it is a chief means of
persuading the reader that Gregor is in the real world. It is his
room with its familiar objects that functions as evidence that he
is not dreaming:

'Was ist mit mir geschehen?' dachte er. Es war kein
Traum. Sein Zimmer, ein richtiges, nur etwas zu kleines
Menschenzimmer, lag ruhig zwischen den vier wohl-
bekannten Wänden ... (p.19)

Yet this room and its contents are never given firm shape.
Individual objects seem real and solid enough, but the scene as a
whole remains rather imprecise. Gregor's room itself is first
called small, later it is high and roomy (p.38); later still it is said
to be warm (p.49). It contains, it seems, both a bed and a couch
('Kanapee'), though the two might conceivably be the same.
Similarly the table and the desk ('Schreibtisch') might just be

one and the same object. There is at least one chair (called a 'Stuhl' or 'Sessel', the two words are synonymous in Kafka's Austrian German, see the sentence (p.60) where both occur), perhaps several; also at least one cupboard or wardrobe ('Kasten'). The room has wallpaper and a carpet or rug, a picture on the wall; the window looks on to the street and a hospital opposite. There are three doors. One, at the head of the bed, leads to the hall ('Vorzimmer'). The others connect with adjoining rooms. One is the living and dining-room. The other is the sister's room, later used by the parents after they have given up their room beyond the living-room to the lodgers; at this stage the sister sleeps in the living-room. All four rooms must be on one side of the hall. On the other side, we may assume, is the kitchen.[5] But such facts are treated rather nonchalantly and the total picture remains rather vague and must be deduced from isolated statements.

Such an appartment, with windows whose double glazing is set in two separate frames, with interconnecting rooms separated by double doors (i.e. doors with two opening wings), can still be found in older dwellings in Europe. The lock whose key turns several times is also a continental phenomenon. Such details are recognisably real. That the living-room is lit by gas, though there is electric lighting in the streets and an electric tram, places the story in an era. It is a time when an impoverished middle-class family could employ at least one maid so that mother and daughter would be unused to cooking and housework, and when the respectable bourgeois would not forget his hat and walking stick. The strongbox made by the Wertheim firm, and the elaborately carved furniture in the living-room, further reinforce the period flavour. All in all there is no reason to doubt that this is a 'real' appartment in a town within the Austrian Empire and that the time is the early twentieth century. But the town and the year are not named, and how characteristic it is that the street name like the name of Gregor's sister slips out as if by chance (p.44). For all the details crop up disconnectedly, as in a dream.

[5] Beicken, *11*, p.119, produces a plan of the flat.

The piecemeal releasing of potentially significant facts is a marked characteristic of Kafka's technique. It is to be seen also in revelations about Gregor's past life which could be of great importance in explaining his metamorphosis. All this frustrates the reader's desire for explanation. Is not this gradual, seemingly haphazard revelation of facts and the shrouding of the complete picture in mystery part of a consistent narrative strategy? Something is certainly gained by it. Separate objects assume a certain solidity or life of their own. That may testify to the author's accurate observation of reality, as when the rain is said to fall 'nur mit großen, einzeln sichtbaren und förmlich auch einzelnweise auf die Erde hinuntergeworfenen Tropfen' (p.31). But, as in a detective novel before the identity of the criminal is revealed, individual facts or objects, especially those mentioned several times, seem to beckon as clues. The objects seem to attract symbolic significance which must be linked to the circumstances and mentality of the hero and ultimately to the metamorphosis itself.

A great many of the vagaries in the manner in which Gregor's new body and the setting are described do indeed become meaningful as renderings of the experience of one who comes to know this body gradually, who registers its gradual deterioration, who has little interest in unobtrusive servants, and no need to establish details about a flat he knows very well. The story makes much more sense once it is recognised that its events are seen largely through the eyes of Gregor Samsa, through a mind blinkered by its own moods and expectations, a mind that does not even ask, let alone answer, the question of meaning which intrigues the reader.

2. Perspectives

When someone recounts an event he can give a personal colouring to his account and the listener allows for that colouring, discounts it as evident bias or enjoys it as added interest. Sometimes, of course, the account has through the standing of the reporter the stamp of impartiality. It is such impartiality which we normally expect of an author in his role as narrator of a work of fiction. Indeed we are ready to accept in such a narrator an omniscience which would not be credible in a witness to the events narrated. Even when the narrator's knowledge is more restricted and in keeping with normal human limitations we accept him as an absolute authority for the purposes of the story.

The writer who wishes to present the experiences of one character may, however, choose to write in the first person as if he were that character. The account may then be more vivid, intense and lifelike. It can throw a special light on a problem even if its subjectivity is manifest. Yet the chief character who is also the narrator cannot, unless he is to seem unusually introspective or to be granted privileged hindsight, enjoy too much self-knowledge. Where motivation at less than a fully conscious level is to be explored the impersonal narrator has an advantage. He can claim both to understand and to judge.

In the previous chapter I was concerned with the activity of the author who as narrator arranges his material. This narrator is an impersonal one; he remains completely anonymous. So little perceptible is he indeed that some critics have denied his very existence, except in the epilogue. Yet, strangely, he is not a dispassionate onlooker; for he tells the story as if he were the hero, and is almost indistinguishable from him. He achieves the vividness of first-person narrative while yet avoiding the first-person singular. Since he does not claim any understanding of the events superior to that of his hero it is not immediately clear what advantage he gains from the third-person form, except the ability to tell of events after the hero's death. That one justification may, of course, be significant as a pointer to the supreme importance of the epilogue. But we may immediately note that in essence investigation of the narrative perspective promises or threatens to confirm my earlier conclusions: the use of the third person and of the past tense leads the reader to expect a reliability of vision, but the figural perspective (to which I now turn) thwarts that expectation.

In *Die Verwandlung* the emphasis is on impact, not explanation. Things are mentioned as and when they impinge on the hero's mind, as they are needed to further the narrative, and not necessarily when they are needed to facilitate the reader's full understanding of the situation. The technique used to achieve this perspective is by no means obtrusive.

In the opening paragraph the figural perspective is scarcely noticeable. The 'fand er sich' (rather than 'war er') of the first sentence passes unremarked. It can, like the adjectives in the first paragraph, and like the phrase 'sah, wenn er den Kopf ein wenig hob', function as an authorial statement independent of the subjectivity of the hero. The second paragraph is no different, for when Gregor's thoughts are given they are clearly signalled as his thoughts. Only at the start of the third paragraph does the word 'dann' indicate that the description follows Gregor's gaze. And only much later is it apparent that 'ein richtiges, nur etwas zu kleines Menschenzimmer' is not necessarily a reliably objective statement. If the room is now said to be too small, it is because Gregor would have liked different accommodation. The hint that he has not been satisfied with his lot will soon be confirmed when his thoughts turn to his job.

Throughout the story, most particularly at the points of climax, and most frequently in the first section, there are indications that the narrator records what Gregor sees. Gregor directs his gaze (p.19) or his eyes (p.24), he raises his head (pp.19, 53), exchanges glances (p.62), he casts sideways glances (p.35), observes (pp.39, 51), or has no time to watch (p.34), he complains about a sight (p.59), and, of course, he sees or looks at something (pp.19, 20, 23, 31, 34, 37, 40, 46, 51, 54, 57, 67,

68). From his first sight of himself to his last view of his mother
and his questioning look around in the darkness of his room a
few hours before his death, the angle of vision does not change.
If his father's boots have gigantic soles (p.53) it is not because he
has enormous feet, but because the panic-stricken Gregor sees
them from his position close to the floor. Of course Gregor
hears much too; voices and noises carry easily through the flat.
Thus he gathers what is happening outside his room and what
has happened unnoticed by him. He interprets what he sees and
hears and it is his interpretation that is given. Occasionally the
sounds are obviously exaggerated in his mind: the 'möbel-
erschütterndes Läuten' of the alarm (p.21), for instance, or the
voice of his father — 'es klang ... gar nicht mehr wie die Stimme
bloß eines einzigen Vaters' (p.36). But generally thoughts and
feelings merge with the narrative and become part of it. Quite
often the narrator signals that he is reporting Gregor's thoughts
and questions. Even when not signalled they cannot always be
mistaken for the narrator's own utterances. But often too they
can function as either the narrator's or Gregor's observations.
Who is it for instance who asks the rhetorical question, 'Wer
hatte in dieser abgearbeiteten und übermüdeten Familie Zeit,
sich um Gregor mehr zu kümmern, als unbedingt nötig war?'
(p.57); or the equally loaded question, 'War er ein Tier, da ihn
Musik so ergriff?' (p.63)? As the adverbs reveal, the narrator
vouches only for that which seems probable or beyond question
to the hero:

Infolge der Holztür war die Veränderung in Gregors
Stimme draußen wohl nicht zu merken, denn ... (p.22)

offenbar führte sie die Mutter an der Hand (p.48)

Gewiß wollten auch sie nicht, daß Gregor verhungerte
(p.40)

Dem Vater fiel es natürlich in seiner gegenwärtigen
Verfassung auch nicht entfernt ein, etwa den anderen
Türflügel zu öffnen (p.35)

Only on reflection is it apparent that the words 'man sah'
(pp.21, 31, 65) are simply variations on the recurrent 'er sah'
and that neither guarantees objective vision.

Through the narrative perspective the reader experiences the
events as vividly and as confusedly as Gregor Samsa. He also
shares the hero's awareness of time. The first section covers less
than an hour. Shortly after waking Gregor notices that it is
already past six thirty. The alarm clock was set at four and he
should have caught the five-o'clock train. He can hardly now
catch the seven-o'clock train, for before he can even get out of
bed it is six forty-five. Indeed time flies, it is ten past seven when
the chief clerk arrives, and he is still in bed. From then on the
time is not mentioned, for Gregor is in no state to look at a clock
again, but it is clear that the events described occupy only a few
minutes. In this first part Gregor is still thinking in terms of the
exactly measured time of an overworked and anxious travelling
salesman given to studying timetables even in his free time. But
he cannot now re-enter the world of work in which time is
money and punctuality a necessity and a virtue. He has missed
the train; this first 'Versäumnis' (p.21) entails, as the chief clerk
reminds him, a failure in his duty as an employee — 'Sie ...
versäumen ... Ihre gesellschaftlichen Pflichten' (p.27). Then he
is accused of wasting the chief clerk's time ('da Sie mich hier
meine Zeit versäumen lassen' (p.28)). In the second section there
is no reference to the clock time of regulated modern life, only to
the time of day, to the passing of weeks and months. The
chronology becomes blurred and the narrative departs from the
strict sequence of events. Before the second dramatic confrontation with his family two months have elapsed. The last section
begins one month after the end of the second; during this last
phase Gregor notices that Christmas has probably passed — he
has missed the festive season just as he missed the train. The
metamorphosis took place before Christmas, when the weather
suggested late autumn or early winter. Finally, it seems that
spring is approaching. Only in the epilogue is the month firmly
established: Gregor dies at the end of March.

Gregor's failure to keep track of time is symptomatic of his
condition. There is no mention of any attempts by him to con-

sult or wind up his alarm clock or of his missing it after his furniture is removed. Nor does he attempt to keep a record of the passing of days in the time-honoured prisoner's way of making marks on wall or floor. But the reader is not encouraged to imagine that Gregor is negligent, rather to believe that the hero cannot be expected to notice exactly the passing of the hours, days and weeks. Indeed the impression is given that Gregor's diminishing awareness of time, his uselessness — his inability to make good use of time — and the gradual slowing down of his movements, even the diminution of any urge to live, are all connected and have been forced upon him; this even though his every first thoughts after his transformation are concerned with a reluctance to bestir himself and to be ruled by the time demands of his job. The narrator's initial insistence on time and his subsequent failure to document it are evidently deliberate.

For the narrator is not completely absent, though his presence is discreet. Occasionally, even before Gregor's death, he speaks with his own voice. It is he who on the first page explains in parenthesis that his hero is a travelling salesman. It is he who tells us what his hero is not thinking:

> Und ohne daran zu denken, daß er seine gegenwärtigen Fähigkeiten, sich zu bewegen, noch gar nicht kannte, ohne auch daran zu denken, daß seine Rede möglicher- ja wahrscheinlicherweise wieder nicht verstanden worden war, verließ er den Türflügel (p.33)

It is the narrator who reminds us that Gregor's apparent intention to advise his sister is quite unrealistic (p.51) and points out Gregor's lack of consideration — of which, it is said, the hero is hardly aware (p.63) and of which, we might think, he is probably not conscious at all. Above all he reports Gregor's thoughts and feelings, often with a sustained literary articulateness of which his hero seems scarcely capable; and he determines the perspective, and blurs the distinction between the narrator's voice and that of his hero. It is Kafka as narrator who notes that the third hour strikes as Gregor lies dying — this despite the

danger that his reader may ask why Gregor has not heard this
clock striking outside before. The narrator, too, decides on the
allocation of light and dark, of gloomy weather and sunshine,
features which assume a symbolic significance beyond that of a
reflection of Gregor's state of mind. For symbolism of light and
weather continues beyond Gregor's death, indeed becomes
unmistakable in the epilogue when for the first time in the story
the sun shines warmly.

The symbolism is telling. Gregor is cut off from the light in
the living-room, from contact with his family and inclusion in
'den menschlichen Kreis' (p.29). He is separated from the
human world by a locked door, or when the door is left open he
is not expected to cross the threshold. He is separated from the
light of day outside, from the possibility of escape which the
window had once seemed to promise him (p.44): the window
now gives little light and no cheer, indeed it reveals only a
uniform greyness. Yet for his sister it provides, as a means to
fresh air, real relief. The window in the living-room has an
identical physical and symbolic function for the mother: she
leans far out of it to recover from shock. After Gregor's death
the charwoman opens the casement and lets in fresh air, and
later mother and sister stand together at the window. The door
as a barrier has a significance for all the characters. Its key is a
means of control. The manipulation of such symbolism is the
narrator's doing. Thus the use of the words 'Versäumnis' and
'versäumen' to link time with work and duty to others is of his
choosing; they are put into the thoughts and speech of Gregor
(p.21), his mother (p.26) and the chief clerk (pp.27, 28) as if to
indicate that there are concerns or preconceptions common to
Gregor and the others. The hero's viewpoint may not be so subjective after all when it comes to values and aims.

In the epilogue the characters known previously as the father
and mother are consistently referred to as Herr Samsa and Frau
Samsa, and the sister, Grete, becomes the daughter. Yet despite
the change of perspective some symbolic patterns are continued
and indeed the ending owes much of its effectiveness to that.
Now the narrator confidently tells of the thoughts of the charwoman alone with Gregor's corpse, of Herr Samsa's distrust of

the lodgers and his anxiety in checking that they really leave the flat, of the thoughts of Herr and Frau Samsa in the tram and the looks they exchange 'fast unbewußt' (p.73). He is able to move from the consciousness of the charwoman to that of the parents. Yet he does not claim omniscience. He can, it seems, only guess at the thoughts and feelings of the lodgers; he does not guarantee that Grete has not slept but only gives evidence suggesting that she has not. He seems to watch the charwoman coming to report the removal of Gregor's body as if he were one of the family present in the room and yet to see the Samsas from without as they act in unison and become an undifferentiated 'man' (p.71). It is not clear whether he confirms the Samsas' opinion that they deserve as well as need a day's rest from work. Curiously he does not even vouch for the fact that they are relieved to see the lodgers leave ('wie erleichtert' (p.71)). It is, however, clear that the family is relieved as well as saddened by Gregor's death. But the narrator does not claim to be privy to all their thoughts and emotions. He does not pass judgment on the characters. The impersonal narrator has revealed his presence, he has become less furtive, but he offers no complete explanations and does not tell his reader what to think.

Because at least some of the apparently or obviously symbolic features of this story recur in the epilogue and thus transcend the viewpoint of the hero they seem doubly significant. The need to transcend that viewpoint is felt if only because Gregor's understanding is noticeably restricted. He is very slow to take in the inevitable consequences of his metamorphosis. While that slowness is not surprising, given the circumstances, it also reflects a mind subconsciously intent on evading reality and vacillating illogically between irreconcilable lines of action. On the one hand he wants to go back to sleep and forget everything, on the other he admits the necessity of going to work. He dreams of quitting his job, and insists that he is intent on keeping it. He attempts to disguise his animal voice so as not to worry his family yet then subjects them to the sight of his body half in the hope that they will calmly accept his new shape. When his feet begin to obey him he believes in the possibility of an immediate 'endgültige Besserung' (p.34). He quite ludicrously claims for himself a quality of foresight that he denies his parents. On the first evening he seems not to conceive of the likelihood that the family's habits have changed suddenly since that morning rather than 'in der letzten Zeit' (p.37). His evident misunderstanding of his sister's actions in the second section reinforces this impression that Gregor is incapable of proper insight, and his violent change of mind about the clearance of his room underlines his lack of logical consistency and of self-knowledge. In the third section he still thinks, quite unrealistically, of assuming charge of family affairs once more. Even his sense of humour, evident when he dismisses as idle any notion of others assisting him out of his bed, is clearly out of place. Misplaced too, and symptomatic of a tendency to platitude, are the insect's words of wisdom and self-encouragement, 'Der Mensch muß seinen Schlaf haben' (p.20) and 'Nur sich nicht im Bett unnütz aufhalten' (p.23). Gregor is, furthermore, in his confusion and panic, capable of lies and self-contradiction, as when he calls to the chief clerk in the neighbouring room (p.28).

Irrelevance and inadequacy of reaction, understandable in the circumstances, are not confined to Gregor. The mother's dwelling on Gregor's pastimes is obviously irrelevant to the concerns of the chief clerk, and the father's musings on the impossibility of reaching an understanding with Gregor illustrate his inadequacy too. But signs of Gregor's inadequacy are perhaps more significant in that they can both increase sympathy for him and encourage a more distanced view of his state. Such detachment on the part of the reader is encouraged by and facilitates the recognition of irony or humour in the story. There is an irony in the deliberate exaggeration of emotions, or perhaps more accurately a playfulness in Kafka's choice of a scenario in which no reaction seems either exaggerated or appropriate. The word 'Menschenzimmer' on the first page can be taken as a wryly amusing formation (on the basis of 'Kinderzimmer'). Certainly there is humour in Gregor's realisation that he has 'keine rechte Vorstellung' (p.23) of his new body just after he has been thinking how 'seine heutigen Vorstellungen' (p.22) will disappear, convinced that the change in his voice is simply the sign of a cold; potential comedy too, in the flight of the chief clerk, the slow chase of Herr Samsa and the insect round the living room, or in the notion that the widowed charwoman has survived the vicissitudes of life 'mit Hilfe ihres starken Knochenbaus' (p.59). The last example has more point if it is allowed that it is Gregor who formulates the thought and that he as an insect has no proper bones. Certainly he accuses a menial in his firm of lacking the 'Rückgrat und Verstand' (p.21) that he presumably lacks himself. Kafka, reading from *Die Verwandlung* to his friends, did so with abandon, but he seems not to have been surprised or hurt that the reading was followed by general laughter (BrF., p.320). Do not caricaturists often present a human being as an animal?

There is a certain parody of the individuals who are reduced to a function or to automatons, of the chief clerk who cannot quite bring himself to defend Gregor with full conviction ('ich legte wahrhaftig fast mein Ehrenwort dafür ein' (p.27)), of the lodgers and the business-like charwoman. The absence of ambiguity in these figures is some relief, for in them we sense a world in which the problems of the Samsas are of little concern. Yet neither lodgers nor charwoman nor the three surviving Samsas are associated unequivocally with attitudes or values more positive than those of Gregor, and the narrator does not identify with them. The sense of relief is not complete. The comic relief afforded by the incongruity between Gregor's thoughts and behaviour and the reality of his situation remained a possibility rather than a certainty, for it could also serve to intensify the horror. Irony underlined the incompleteness of Gregor's understanding, but it did not originate in the narrator's confident possession of a superior alternative. The more objective alternative which the main patterns of symbolism seemed to offer appears itself to be ironised in the epilogue. The movement from darkness into light, from despair to hope, confinement to freedom, decay and death to new life, rather too crudely implies a happy ending. The reader who has been forced to share Gregor's point of view cannot switch emotional allegiance so quickly. Nor can he see the hero as a ridiculous caricature. Yet significantly there is irony in the report that when Gregor finally finds himself in complete agreement with his

family his thoughts are empty as well as peaceful. He may at the
moment of death recall his family 'mit Rührung und Liebe'
(p.68) but the story has shown the failure of love.

Any interpretation of *Die Verwandlung*, on whatever level,
must nevertheless rest on some or all of the symbolic patterns in
the story. The characters themselves cannot be judged without
reference to them for they are in large part portrayed through
actions, gestures and motifs which are interrelated. Gregor is not
aware, it seems, of many of these interrelations. His unaware-
ness of them contributes to the suspicion that Kafka as narrator,
in apparently withholding information, is challenging the reader
to find the right perspective from which all will fall into place
within a comprehensible whole.

3. Characters and Relations

Thanks to the narrative perspective the reader more readily sees the father and sister as traitors to the son than as victims of an insect pest. Yet if Gregor's metamorphosis relieves him of responsibility for events, it also explains and excuses the reactions of his family. Moral judgments on father, daughter and son become difficult: one might find them all equally innocent or equally base. For if Gregor's blood relations contrast with him in their discovery of a purposefulness and vitality that are denied him, they share certain of his characteristics. The parallels and contrasts between the characters are confusingly complex and form a thematic labyrinth from which any escape to clear conclusions and judgments is beset with perplexities.

Gregor's mother is the least complicated of his relatives. His picture of her as a gentle, loving but rather helpless person cannot seriously be challenged. She clings to the hope that he will recover from his 'illness' and insists on the importance of giving him to understand that they believe in the possibility of his return to normality (admittedly it may be the magnitude of the task of clearing his room that causes her thus to rationalise her plan not to remove his furniture). She insists that the insect is still her son and longs to see him. She implores her husband to stop bombarding Gregor with apples, and makes as if to stop the charwoman from demonstrating with a thrust of the broom how dead Gregor really is. Gregor clearly sympathises with her. But she is essentially a passive figure who gives in to her husband and daughter. Yet like her husband and daughter she proves unexpectedly capable of work, and this new vitality, though not presented as a transformation, contrasts, together with her constant identification with the family unit, with the fate of Gregor. Her helplessness, her tendency to faint and to cling to unrealistic hope, and her submissiveness are not unlike certain

characteristics in Gregor himself. This partial parallel perhaps
suggests that selfless love is a drain on vital energy akin to illness
(the mother's debility being comparable to Gregor's weariness
which is caused before his metamorphosis by his consciousness
of sacrifice and after it by his inability to express his love). But
unlike Gregor Frau Samsa does not rebel against love as an irk-
some duty. Her distress reminds Gregor of his failure in his
duty.

Most commentators see Gregor's father as violent, aggressive,
selfish and unjust, and find hints of this in his very first actions
and words. His brief question at Gregor's door need, however,
be no different in intent from his wife's: an expression of concern. His voice is raised, yet his knock is soft and he takes no
further action until the chief clerk arrives twenty minutes later.
That he knocks with his fist, rather than taps with his fingers,
need be significant only in so far as it appears threatening to
Gregor. Nor does his sending for a locksmith in itself suggest
violence, it is a practical step necessary if the doctor is to get to
Gregor. Yet Herr Samsa's clenched fist when Gregor appears in
the doorway is clearly a gesture of anger and threat:

> Der Vater ballte mit feindseligem Ausdruck die Faust, als
> wolle er Gregor in sein Zimmer zurückstoßen. (p.31)

The sister, too, raises her fist when Gregor causes their mother
to faint (p.51). The father's clenched fist is also a sign of
emotional tension: he sobs and looks around, unsure what to
do. He offers the chief clerk no excuse for his son's failure to
report for work; but he may reasonably not wish to pre-empt
Gregor's own explanation. His severity towards Gregor, said to
date from the metamorphosis (p.53), is in itself no crime. It
involves a lack of understanding not surprising in the circumstances, but not tyranny or injustice. The impression that Herr
Samsa is violent and cruel rests on his actions in driving Gregor
back into his room. But again his loss of composure which
Gregor expects and yet finds reprehensible is not unnatural in
the circumstances. Gregor, in his panic, seems to exaggerate the
violence of his father's intention. Gregor and the narrative voice

do not appear to allow for the father's fear for himself and for
the womenfolk, nor for his understandable failure to recognise
the insect's intention of retreating meekly. Nor is his reaction on
Gregor's second breakout so terribly reprehensible. Having
warned the women not to risk a confrontation of Gregor and his
mother — 'mit Vernunftgründen, die er [Gregor] vollständig
billigte' (p.46) — he is partly gratified that his warning was justi-
fied: 'gleichzeitig wütend und froh' (p.53). He is frustrated when
Gregor retreats before him and both circle meaninglessly round
the room. Gregor cannot be driven back into his room as long as
the mother is there. In his frustration the father seriously
wounds Gregor. But Gregor himself is incapable of logical
thought or meaningful action at this time, for he too believes
that the mother's life is in danger. The father has assumed
hostility in Gregor. He like his wife has awaited signs of
improvement in Gregor and has praised Grete's efforts in caring
for him (p.46). He is not consistently hostile to Gregor. Indeed
at the end he is less aggressive than Grete. He seems to have con-
cluded that they must suffer the presence of the horror in the flat
(p.55). At the final climax, in contrast to his decisive treatment
of the lodgers, he makes no attempt to get rid of Gregor, but
simply remarks that there is no possiblity of reaching an understanding with him. As a response to his daughter's outburst,
which is also a plea for help, that is rather tame. He seems to
reveal a desire for a peaceful solution. He is described as
impatient (p.26), and indeed he is on occasions. He rebukes both
women when they quarrel about who should be responsible for
Gregor's room (p.59). Gregor is also angered by the same
quarrel. Both men want to be left in peace. Herr Samsa did not
reveal that he had enough money to have paid some of the debt
to Gregor's employer and have shortened the time Gregor
needed to continue in the job he disliked. Such secrecy was
unfair to Gregor, even though he accepts that in view of his
metamorphosis the father's action was fortunate or prudent.
But that secrecy must be weighed against Gregor's uncommuni-
cativeness: Herr Samsa did not know that his son was unhappy
in his job. The parents assumed that he was settled in it for life
(p.33). Gregor envied those who like his father could lead a life of

leisure. Yet he soon discovers that enforced idleness is humiliating: an experience that his father may well have had on his retirement. If Gregor the breadwinner seems to have regarded his father as a parasite, he also recognised that he had, before the bankruptcy, never taken a break in the course of a long and hard working life.

More damning, perhaps, than anything the father does is what he does not do: he does not enter Gregor's room from the time of his metamorphosis until his death. That must be significant in a story in which attempts to help and make contact are identified with traffic between Gregor's room and the rest of the flat. Sister and mother come into Gregor's room, Gregor goes into the living-room. Herr Samsa may, it seems, hope for Gregor's improvement but he does not attempt to help him. He remains aloof, and that aloofness may be interpreted as condemnation. The suspicion that he at some level of consciousness welcomes the opportunity to re-establish his lost authority cannot be lightly dismissed. (Gregor has since his father's retirement assumed the role of head of family; he chose the flat.) But then aloofness and enjoyment of status characterised Gregor the breadwinner. Rashness, apparent aggression, jumping to conclusions characterise Gregor the insect as well as his father. They have much in common. It seems that Gregor may have inherited from his parents contradictory traits — or that aspects of his personality are exteriorised in the figures of the parents. Herr Samsa's apparent acceptance that they must suffer the presence of Gregor as a painful duty mirrors Gregor's half-hearted conviction that he must do his job as a duty to his family. To a large extent the two exchange roles.

If Gregor's view of his father is coloured by fear, anger and guilt, and if he is surprised by his regeneration, he is similarly blinkered in his view of his sister. He thinks of her as a spoilt child, despite her seventeen years, but is proudly possessive about her. She was his real contact with the family. Through her he learnt what was happening at home while he was away (p.37). He believes she is on his side. Her weeping on the arrival of the chief clerk he interprets as a sign of intelligent sympathy. He regrets that she is not present later to charm the chief clerk on his behalf. On the first evening he immediately assumes that it is she who brings him his favourite drink. The next day she provides him 'in ihrer Güte' with a selection of food:

> Und aus Zartgefühl, da sie wußte, daß Gregor vor ihr nicht essen würde, entfernte sie sich eiligst und drehte sogar den Schlüssel um, damit nur Gregor merken könne, daß er es sich so behaglich machen dürfe, wie er wolle. (p.39)

This must be Gregor's interpretation of her motives, for her actions speak more strongly of fear or repulsion. Despite his disappointment that even she does not imagine that he can still understand the language of humans he continues to feel grateful for her kindness. It seems that he thinks she leaves the secondary window open for his sake rather than to facilitate the wrenching open of the window as soon as she enters. Eventually he realises that the sight of him fills her with fear and disgust (pp.45-46). Consequently he is critical of her refusal to share the care of him with his mother and ascribes her service to him to childish thoughtlessness rather than real love. During the furniture removal he sees in her not just a new self-confidence, but possessiveness, selfishness and the stubbornness of a teenage girl. A few minutes later, when Frau Samsa faints, Grete has become an enemy. She raises her fist and glares as she addresses her first words — the angry 'Du, Gregor!' — to him since his metamorphosis (p.51). This happens just after he has stubbornly defied her:

> Er saß auf seinem Bild und gab es nicht her. Lieber würde er Grete ins Gesicht springen. (p.51)

The aggression is mutual, and like that between Gregor and his father, it is based on a lack of mutual understanding. For Grete's plan to empty Gregor's room is contrary to his interests only if there is hope that the presence of his furniture will help him regain his human form. She cannot consult him about his wishes, but he did not consider it necessary to discuss with her his plans for her musical education. Grete wishes to make him as happy as possible and to remove much of the burden of care from their parents; her plan stands parallel to his earlier intentions towards her and the parents. It perhaps has the merit of realism. Any selfishness in her love for him is later surpassed by his dream of having her all to himself. Just as her enthusiasm for ministering to him wanes when the novelty of the task wears off, so did Gregor's enthusiasm for providing for the family. Gregor's assessment, 'sie war klug' (p.33), finds its ironic vindication in the last part of the story. Her conclusion, 'wir müssen versuchen, es loszuwerden' (p.66), reflects a new-found assertiveness. But it is also born of frustration and despair. As the one who has been most exposed to the horrid reality of the 'sick' and apparently ungrateful Gregor, Grete not unnaturally feels impelled to pronounce on the inhuman demands of the task. Given that he is undoubtedly repulsive and that no understanding with him is possible there is truth in her conclusion:

'Wir haben das Menschenmögliche versucht, es zu pflegen und zu dulden, ich glaube, es kann uns niemand den geringsten Vorwurf machen'. (p.66)

Gregor apparently does not see that she, like him, but more decisively and consciously, has rebelled against an unpleasant duty. Their estrangement cannot obscure the fact that her verdict on the impossibility of their relationship becomes his verdict and was even possibly one that he was waiting for someone to formulate:

Seine Meinung darüber, daß er verschwinden müsse, war womöglich noch entschiedener als die seiner Schwester. (p.68)

It is the logical consequence of an attitude that was associated with the father. For Grete too is the child of her parents; but instead of wavering between the attitudes of each like Gregor, she represents in heightened form that of the mother and then that of the father. The condemnation of Gregor was latent in his very presence as a son and brother who is less than human. The contrast between her transformation and his — the one brings integration into the world of work and family, the other utter alienation from both — appears to reflect two warring dispositions within Gregor himself. For both before his metamorphosis and immediately after it he loves his family and yet resents their demands on him. The same conflict is experienced by Grete — and by Herr Samsa, who with the words, 'Das ist ein Leben. Das ist die Ruhe meiner alten Tage' (p.56), complains of his exertions on behalf of the family and yet enjoys the approval they bring.

Communication, understanding, love, isolation, suspicion, resentment and hatred are aspects of interhuman relationships and of the strength or weakness of a social unit. In *Die Verwandlung* physical proximity and contact between individuals indicate degrees of identification with the family. Thus Grete moves from apparent isolation into greater association with first her mother and then her father until all three are one at the end.

But there is another group in the story, the lodgers whose presence shows how the three Samsas are reduced to service to others in their need to support themselves without Gregor's income. This service is seen as humiliating, even degrading, comparable to Gregor's former service to the family and to his employer. The lodgers appear as usurpers. They occupy the parents' bedroom, use the living-room while the Samsas retire to the kitchen, they take the places at table formally occupied by the parents and Gregor. They assume that because they are paying they deserve respect. They stand for a certain scale of values asociated both with the power of money and with order and cleanliness and respectability. According to these bourgeois values the filthy insect must indeed represent 'widerliche Verhältnisse' (p.65). For the metamorphosed Gregor has disrupted the established routine. His father apologises for the 'Unordnung' to be expected in Gregor's room (p.26) and it is soon clear that 'es mit ihm nicht ganz in Ordnung war' (p.29). His transformation has put an end to 'alle Ruhe, aller Wohlstand, alle Zufriedenheit' (p.37) in the home. Gregor's first sight of his mother after his metamorphosis is of a woman whose hair is in disorder. On his emergence from his room coffee is upset, papers blow about the room. Gregor himself is from the first conscious of the need to re-establish 'Ruhe und Ordnung' (p.23) in the movement of his legs and in his thoughts and actions:

> Zunächst wollte er ruhig und ungestört aufstehen (p.22)

> ... vergaß er nicht, ... daß viel besser als verzweifelte Entschlüsse ruhige und ruhigste Überlegung sei. (p.23)

The lodgers' discovery of his presence — he advances, covered with filth, on to the spotless floor of the living-room — is reason enough for them to express moral shock and to justify breaking their financial agreement with the Samsas. Gregor shares something of their attitude towards order as a virtue. He resents his family's failure to maintain his room in good order.

The liberation of the family from the burden and shame of Gregor's presence is marked by the charwoman's announcement, 'es ist schon in Ordnung' (p.72). It is accompanied by their dismissal of lodgers and charwoman and thus of tangible links with their suffering and the unwelcome intrusion into their peace. For lodgers and charwoman have lacked proper feeling for the family as well as for Gregor. In freeing themselves from dependence on others (except the dependence on their employers which they do not feel as such a burden) the Samsas achieve as a group that self-sufficiency which Gregor must have dreamt of attaining for himself alone. He too has been insensitive to family feelings, and he too might be accused of having attempted to usurp a position of authority and respect in his role as breadwinner.

The portrayal of the lodgers indicates that a harmonious grouping of people can be far from ideal. These men share too much, their appearance and habits as well as the same newspaper. The only individuality noticeable among them is that one of the three consistently acts as leader and spokesman. But he proves no match for Herr Samsa. Unlike Gregor this leader is quick to recognise a new order and new hierarchy:

> Herr Samsa ... ging in einer Linie mit seinen zwei
> Begleiterinnen auf den Zimmerherrn zu. Dieser stand
> zuerst still da und sah zu Boden, als ob sich die Dinge in
> seinem Kopf zu einer neuen Ordnung zusammenstellten.
> "Dann gehen wir also", sagte er ... (p.70)

(Here again calmness and order are closely related. Earlier the
two other lodgers had rubbed their hands in excited anticipation,
and all three plucked 'unruhig' at their beards during the
previous evening's confrontation with Herr Samsa (p.64). Now
they listen 'mit langen ruhigen Händen' (p.71).) The father and
the family prove stronger than the lodgers, just as they prove
stronger than Gregor. The lodgers seem to exist in order to eat
and to read newspapers, much as Herr Samsa did; nothing is
said of their work. As a unit they lack individuality and
dynamism. In contrast the family knows inner conflict, rejects
Gregor as a consequence of suffering and emotional
involvement, and eventually proves to have access to an energy
which may be derived from the conflict (though Gregor himself
does not benefit from it in this way) but appears more certainly
to be connected with the emotional ties they share. From this
shared experience grows the hope and vitality which is
represented at the end in Grete who has blossomed 'zu einem
schönen und üppigen Mädchen' (p.73). As she stretches her
body we may be reminded of another body that, shrivelled and
dried, has been swept out of sight:

> Und es war ihnen [den Eltern] wie eine Bestätigung ihrer
> neuen Träume und guten Absichten, als am Ziele ihrer
> Fahrt die Tochter als erste sich erhob und ihren jungen
> Körper dehnte. (p.73)

The Samsas' trip is a journey to freedom and hope; Gregor's
journeys — 'Samsa war Reisender' (p.19) — brought him little
satisfaction, only weariness; his wanderings around his room are
pointless, his excursions into the living-room failures. Perhaps
he unknowingly admits, when speaking to the chief clerk, that
life is essentially a journey — 'das Reisen ist beschwerlich, aber

ich könnte ohne das Reisen nicht leben' (p.32) — and the desire
to avoid exertion is a denial of life itself.

The bustling charwoman recalls the virtue of making good use
of time. No wonder her clatter and her slamming of doors
irritates Gregor, for she is a reminder of his useless idleness.
Similarly the lodgers represent a rebuke to Gregor. Yet, sur-
prisingly perhaps, they are a caricature of Gregor the dutiful
provider of income. Was his life not like theirs one of routine
empty of real emotional meaning, his free time spent reading
timetables and the newspaper? The paper may function as a link
with the wider world of human affairs, but it also shuts the
reader off from personal communication. Indeed the newspaper
may show that Gregor no longer belongs to humanity — the
father shoos him away with it, and an old copy can serve the
insect only as plate and tablecloth. With their teeth and appetites
and demand for respect the lodgers recall Gregor's earlier self.
The analogy between lodgers and Gregor throws doubt on the
value of an existence which Gregor once led. That they suffer
none of his inner conflicts is appropriate if they too represent
but one aspect of his personality, an aspect which in them is
isolated and exaggerated.

For Gregor's state — a human mind in an insect body —
signifies a dreadful disjunction within him. Because he is torn in
at least two directions at once he tends to allow others to decide
which direction he will take and to welcome this as an escape
from responsibility. Thus, he thinks, the reactions of parents
and chief clerk to his appearance will decide matters for him:

> Würden sie erschrecken, dann hatte Gregor keine Verant-
> wortung mehr und konnte ruhig sein. (p.28)

But Gregor cannot escape his need to relate to other people. He
is dependent on others for his food, for his very existence. There
is only a choice between the affirmation of responsibility (which
becomes meaningless to him in his insect form) or pure selfishness. Between his first and last emergence from his room selfishness has asserted itself as his dominant motive. The story insists
on a connection between work and the value of the individual.

Where, as in Gregor's case, there is no work done, leisure becomes idleness and parasitism and affords no pleasure. Status and self-respect are tied to social values. When Gregor notices the transformation in his father, he notices a gain in self-confidence derived from his renewed position as provider of money. That self-confidence is linked with the uniform that he wears continuously as an emblem of his new status. It is a sign of service (in a menial position) but demands respect for the institution it represents. Gregor himself had once enjoyed such respect when he wore a lieutenant's uniform. The photograph of him in his uniform is a reminder of how his parents would like to see him, enjoying the status of belonging to a publicly recognised hierarchy. In his uniform Herr Samsa appears 'immer zu seinem Dienste bereit' (p.56). In contrast Gregor woke up unprepared for his duty: his samples were not packed. Herr Samsa seems ever prepared to respond to 'die Stimme des Vorgesetzten' (p.56); Gregor did not respond to the alarm clock (assuming that it did ring), and refuses with his resounding 'Nein' to allow his superior, the chief clerk, into his room. For Gregor with one half of his mind rejects submission to authority as slavery. He dreams of toppling his boss from his assumed superiority, he despises a fellow employee who is a 'Kreatur des Chefs' (p.21) and grieves to see his family doing everything that 'die Welt von armen Leuten verlangt' (p.57).

Much of Gregor's behaviour implies a regression into early childhood. He becomes completely reliant on others for food and is incapable of keeping his room and himself clean. Like a child he is punished by being confined to his room. He tells lies in a desperate effort to justify himself. He hides under the bed and plans to steal from the larder. And he must continually look up to his father. Emotional deprivation is not new to him. He has not developed relationships with people outside his family. His memories of colleagues at work and of 'zwei, drei Freunde aus anderen Geschäften' (p.58) are without warmth. His relations with women apart from his mother and sister seem to have been almost as insignificant, except that the thought of a certain shop-girl is linked with consciousness of failure: he wooed her without sufficient urgency (p.58). It remains unclear

how far such immaturity is imposed upon him by circumstances.
While his earnings go to keep the family and to pay his father's
debt he can hardly contemplate marriage.

Gregor resents the uncongenial work expected of him and
would prefer to choose his own way of life. Yet to reject the role
he is expected to play entails forfeiting claims to respect and
love. He seems to have no clear notion of how otherwise to
justify his existence. He is incapable of finding satisfaction in
that which nourishes others, yet alternative sources of nourishment and ultimately of the strength to continue living prove
either unsatisfying (the leftovers) or unobtainable presumably
because they are purely spiritual or beyond his experience (the
unknown 'Nahrung' (p.63) apparently promised by his sister's
music). Gregor is not wholehearted about anything, he can never
be either an authority or a rebel. He is the victim of a guilt that
he only half accepts. He feels guilty about his job because his
heart is not in it, indeed he implies that his metamorphosis is a
consequence of guilt feelings:

> Waren denn alle Angestellten samt und sonders Lumpen,
> gab es denn unter ihnen keinen treuen, ergebenen
> Menschen, der, wenn er auch nur ein paar Morgenstunden
> für das Geschäft nicht ausgenützt hatte, vor Gewissens-
> bissen närrisch wurde und geradezu nicht imstande war,
> das Bett zu verlassen? (p.25)

Shortly after this, however, he asserts his innocence, accuses
others of judging him wrongly and sees himself as suffering 'am
eigenen Leibe' (p.32) the results of this injustice. Both of these
explanations of Gregor's metamorphosis are, in realistic terms,
impossible. Common to both is the assumption that mental
events can determine the physical world. That assumption,
indeed, underlies the story as a whole. Gregor recovers quickly
from his first injuries; the second wound remains and hurts most
when he shares the misery of his relatives (p.57); the final
'wounding' is purely mental and proves fatal. It seems
reasonable to suppose that, just as by a huge extension of the
pathetic fallacy, space, time and light become functions of the

hero's state of soul, so his physical injuries mark psychological wounds which increase in severity partly through repetition; and that the metamorphosis itself corresponds to a mental or emotional condition which has to do with Gregor's opinion of himself as well as the actual and imagined opinions of his family about him.

Gregor shows real attachment to his mother and sister as well as anger and resentment. Yet his attachment to the pin-up in his room appears to show how his feeling is misdirected. Making the frame for the picture is the only creative use he is reported to have made of his private hours. Maybe for that reason his possession of it comes in his mind to stand for an important part of his humanity. But his clasp of it seems too passionate and physical. As in the matter of food, so in the sexual sphere, to be human appears to involve animal characteristics:

> [er] preßte sich an das Glas, das ihn festhielt und seinem heißen Bauch wohltat. Dieses Bild wenigstens, das Gregor jetzt ganz verdeckte, würde nun gewiß niemand wegnehmen ... er klebte ... fest an dem Glas und mußte sich mit Gewalt losreißen (p.51)

The impression of unnatural heat is given later too when Gregor imagines himself protecting his sister from all comers:

> Er wollte sie nicht mehr aus seinem Zimmer lassen, wenigstens nicht, solange er lebte; seine Schreckgestalt sollte ihm zum erstenmal nützlich werden; an allen Türen seines Zimmers wollte er gleichzeitig sein und den Angreifern entgegenfauchen ... Gregor würde sich bis zu ihrer Achsel erheben und ihren Hals küssen, den sie, seitdem sie ins Geschäft ging, frei ohne Band oder Kragen trug. (p.64)

Gregor's love for his sister, an important part of his feeling for the family, turns out to be not only possessive but also potentially incestuous.

Does this mean that human feelings are necessarily contradictory feelings? The contrast between the Samsas and the lodgers might suggest this, and yet the most blatantly self-contradictory figure, Gregor himself, appears as an animal who is an affront to humanity. Is submissiveness a humiliating weakness or a necessary affirmation of group cohesion? Is service to others slavery or does it accord worth to the individual who has no value on his own? How much self-interest and how much altruism is entailed in accepting responsibility and taking charge of others, in assuming and exercising authority? In matters of mutual relations Kafka seems reluctant or unable to decide on ultimate values and to apportion blame. Characteristically the decline of a meaningful interchange into a mechanical routine is described as if it were no one's fault: mutual pleasure and excitement over Gregor's role as breadwinner and debt-payer simply fade with time:

> Man hatte sich daran gewöhnt, sowohl die Familie als auch Gregor, man nahm das Geld dankbar an, er lieferte es gerne ab, aber eine besondere Wärme wollte sich nicht mehr ergeben. (p.42)

The narrator who does not claim to understand everything cannot set himself up as judge. He establishes a few facts, gives his hero's reaction to and interpretation of many of them, and hints at further possible interpretations. The symbolism he uses, whether it involves the movement or position of the characters, doors, windows, communication between people, involves the interpretation of signs. Where the characters do not or cannot express themselves in words their actions and gestures must be read. The movement of eyes becomes particularly significant: the lodger casts his eyes to the floor in a moment of uncertainty or humility (p.70) or looks straight to the front in defiance (p.65). But Gregor's misinterpretation of his sister's actions and gestures and the father's failure to read the body language of the insect serve as warnings that signs may be missed or misconstrued; for to be read properly the individual sign must be placed within a pattern, the right perspective must be gained in order to glimpse the proper meaning and reduce everything to the right order. The proper order of things is, however, precisely what Gregor's metamorphosis, and the *Metamorphosis* as a whole, does not allow. Something has gone wrong with Gregor, with his relation to himself, his family and the world. Or perhaps something is wrong with the family and society, with a world of interrelationships which are complex and contain paradoxes if not contradictions. The story concerns a breakdown of an order which when re-established appears questionable in its very essence. It concerns the desire to help others and be loved and helped by them; and a dream of impossible self-sufficiency; the reward that comes from integration in a human unit; and a desire for freedom. It asks whether spiritual values exist in a world ruled by physical needs and material values, where there is a good measure of selfishness in altruistic attitudes and deeds. It asks to what extent an individual's self-appraisal is determined by the judgment of others, how mind and reality relate to each other, what is real and what is imagination even in those matters which are closest to us. It suggests that the expectation of complete understanding must remain unfulfilled.

4. Samsa and Kafka

'Der Held der Erzählung heißt Samsa', sagte ich. 'Das klingt wie ein Kryptogramm für Kafka. Fünf Buchstaben hier wie dort. Das S im Worte Samsa hat dieselbe Stellung wie das K im Worte Kafka. Das A —' Kafka unterbrach mich.
'Es ist kein Kryptogramm. Samsa ist nicht restlos Kafka. *Die Verwandlung* ist kein Bekenntnis, obwohl es — im gewissen Sinne — eine Indiskretion ist.'[6]

It is scarcely surprising that Kafka was asked, in a conversation recalled here, to confirm and comment on the connection between Gregor Samsa and himself. He himself observed, in a diary entry dated 11 February 1913, a link between the name of the hero of *Das Urteil*, Georg Bendemann, and his own: the first names each of five letters, 'Bende' five letters too like Kafka, with a repeated vowel in the same places, the 'mann' being a suffix, or in Kafka's eyes, a strengthening of it. He can hardly have been unconscious of having chosen, in Samsa, a name even closer to his. Perhaps he based it on the Czech word 'sam' meaning 'alone', that is on a word-play which is hidden even to most Czech speakers. Certainly the similarities between Gregor Samsa and Franz Kafka are many. But they do not amount to a complete identification. *Die Verwandlung* is not a confession, not pure autobiography, though it grew from Kafka's experience and it is this personal involvement that gives the story its emotional urgency. He had experienced the sense of failure, guilt, fear and resentment that is embodied in Gregor.

Gregor's education has been a relatively modest one, concentrating on commercial subjects, whereas Kafka went to a grammar school and studied law at university. He did not work

[6] G. Janouch, *Gespräche mit Kafka: Aufzeichnungen und Erinnerungen* (Frankfurt a.M., Fischer, 1968), p.55.

as a travelling salesman, but as an official in a semi-governmental workers' accident insurance agency. He had not replaced his father as the family's breadwinner. His job did involve occasional journeys to inspect factories, but one real link with Gregor is that Kafka longed to be free of his work but did not have the courage to quit it. He could not envisage other employment that would provide the security and status which were the prerequisites of happiness and self-esteem as defined by contemporary society. There seemed no other, more acceptable means of satisfying his family's expectations of their only son. In a sense, then, although he had been free to choose his own career, his work was forced upon him by his parents and was performed by him as a repellent duty to them. His job tied him to an unwelcome routine. He felt that his time was seldom his own. Above all his job prevented him from devoting all his energies to what he really wanted to do, which was to write. In 1912 he had been working like Gregor for five years (though not for one organisation). Since his heart was not in his work he believed that he did it poorly and felt a secret guilt and a fear of disapproval. In *Die Verwandlung* the chief clerk's accusations of poor performance and misappropriation of funds seem to reflect these, the author's fears. For Kafka exaggerated the crimes against the ethos of work and respectability which he believed others must have seen him committing. They were crimes which, he felt, he must by his very nature involuntarily commit, since he was born to be as useless as Gregor the insect.

Kafka expected to be condemned by others because, ever since he could remember, his own father had viewed him with evident disappointment and disapproval. His father, Hermann Kafka, had worked hard all his life. As a boy, the son of a Yiddish-speaking butcher in a poor village community, he had pushed a pedlar's barrow through the countryside of southern Bohemia. He had moved to Prague, married, opened a shop and taken on employees. Through his own efforts he had risen in the world. He valued such effort all the more because as a Jew he was particularly aware of the need to struggle for security and social status. By sending his son to a German school in Prague Hermann had provided him with the basis for a sound career

which had been denied to those who, like himself, had been
brought up in poverty and in a Czech-speaking backwater of the
Austrian Empire. Franz was expected to build on the success of
his father, to erase memories of the family's background, to
become an important figure within one of the areas of public
life, business or medicine or law, open to Jews. But he did not
fulfil such expectations. He was lacking in self-assertion and in
real concern for the financial success and the prestige that meant
everything to Hermann. He gave no signs of planning an
advantageous marriage. His position in the insurance company
was not well paid. He showed no interest in his father's business,
and Hermann Kafka no interest at all in his son's writing. For he
regarded it as a waste of time and a distraction from the real
business of living. Kafka felt misunderstood, despised and
rejected by his father. Yet he was not confident enough of his
own justification as a person and as a writer to dismiss
altogether his father's judgment which, after all, reflected the
attitudes of most of his fellow men. Indeed one half of Kafka's
being told him that his father was right and his stance was to be
respected and feared. In awe of his father's robust temperament
and physical strength he recognised in him a force to which he
must defer. Looking back on his childhood in the *Brief an den
Vater* he believed that it might have been assumed that his father
would simply stamp on him until nothing of him remained (H.,
p.121) — it is the fear felt by Gregor at the enormous feet of
Herr Samsa. There too he says, 'ich verstummte gänzlich,
verkroch mich vor Dir' and recalls being chased around the table
by his father (H., p.129f.). He wanted to please him. Yet he
knew that his father was insensitive to the feelings of others and
often unjust. He knew that Hermann himself did not identify
with any one of the national or cultural communities of Prague,
Czech, Jewish or German, and, lacking faith in others, suffered
from an insecurity that he bequeathed to his son, but without the
aggressive egotism to counter it. Always Kafka had to compare
himself, and be compared by his father, with his male cousins
who proved their ability to make their way in the world. Two
emigrated to the land of greater opportunity, America. One,
Robert Kafka, was a successful lawyer in Prague. Another,

Ernst Kafka, played a leading part in the expansion of his father's business. A third, Bruno Kafka, made a career as an academic lawyer and later as a politician. The example of another cousin, Oskar Kafka, underlined in a different but no less impressive way the supreme importance of success in the world: he had committed suicide in 1901 when failure in an examination ended his prospects of a promising career in the army. Since Hermann Kafka himself was proud of his own short military service and was disappointed when his young son showed no interest in playing at being a soldier (H., p.123), the photograph of Gregor Samsa as a lieutenant, displayed in the living-room, must have had hurtful personal associations for the author as a sign of expectations not met.

Hermann Kafka worked long hours and had little time to give to his son during the early years which were clearly decisive in forming Franz Kafka's personality and his view of himself, his father, and the world. As an adult his desire not to anger his father meant that he avoided converse with him. Already as a child his awe of his father reduced him to silence: 'ich verlernte das Reden' (H., p.128), was his exaggerated account. The impossibility of communication from which Gregor suffers is based on Kafka's own experience. It is one dimension of that relationship with his father which forms the basis of *Die Verwandlung* as, indeed, according to Kafka himself in 1919, of all his writing: with a clear allusion to *Die Verwandlung*, Kafka said that his father could therefore accuse him of being a parasite (H., p.161).

Gregor's longing for the comfort and encouragement of a visit from his mother seems to echo Kafka's feelings as a child. But like Frau Samsa, Kafka's mother submitted rather passively to her husband's authority. As he explained in the *Brief an den Vater*: 'Zu sehr liebte sie Dich und war Dir zu sehr treu ergeben, als daß sie in dem Kampf des Kindes eine selbständige geistige Macht für die Dauer hätte sein können' (H., p.138). By 1912 he had abandoned hope that she would play a decisive role on his behalf. For she, too, regarded his writing as an activity that he would or should outgrow. While writing *Die Verwandlung* he wrote in a letter:

Ich habe die Eltern immer als Verfolger gefühlt, bis vor
einem Jahr vielleicht war ich gegen sie wie vielleicht gegen
die ganze Welt gleichgültig wie irgendeine leblose Sache,
aber es war nur unterdrückte Angst, Sorge und Traurigkeit
wie ich jetzt sehe. Nichts wollen die Eltern als einen zu sich
hinunterziehen, in die alten Zeiten, aus denen man auf-
atmend aufsteigen möchte, aus Liebe wollen sie es
natürlich, aber das ist ja das Entsetzliche. (BrF., p.112)

He believed that his parents wanted, in their love for him, to
suppress his personality. It seemed to him that they desired a son
who was subservient to their wishes like a small child without a
character of its own, but not a son who is as helpless as an
infant, who like Gregor cannot feed himself or care for himself
or even communicate his wishes and needs; whereas complete
subservience and dependence were inseparable as the opposite of
independent individuality. In 1912, at the age of 29, Kafka felt
that he had failed his parents, but also that he had failed
himself. For he had not freed himself from dependence on them.
He was still living with them, at a time when the eldest of his
younger sisters gave birth to her second child and the next oldest
was about to be married.

The noisy presence of his ten-month-old nephew in his
parents' flat during his sister's confinement served to remind
Kafka that family life was probably incompatible with the peace
he needed in order to write. Yet it was the prospect of marriage
and a family of his own which had occupied Kafka's thoughts
and emotions since meeting Felice Bauer at the home of his
friend, Max Brod, in August 1912. A match with her, a typist
from Berlin, would not be a step up the social scale and therefore could not be expected to please his father. He seems,
indeed, to have suspected that Hermann Kafka did not really
want his son to grow up and to threaten, or free himself from,
his authority. In *Das Urteil* Kafka imagined a father's condemnation of a son who plans to take over the family business
and assume the status of head of family. He had imagined how,
after a reversal of positions of strength similar to the transformations of *Die Verwandlung*, the son carries out the death

sentence passed on him by his father. For the father of Georg
Bendemann speaks to and for that part of his son which clings to
bachelorhood, to the solitary life of an outsider which Kafka
himself suspected he was destined to lead and was necessary for
him as a creative writer. In the five years during which he
struggled with the promise and the threat that Felice meant to
him Kafka wooed her by letter, desperate in his desire for
companionship, with conviction when he lost faith in his
vocation as a writer, but doubtfully at other times; for might not
she represent an end to the peculiar existence dictated to him by
his nature and his muse? Could she possibly agree to take second
place to his writing, would she allow him to live the abnormal
life that any ordinary person condemned? His mother worried
about his diet (his appetite was small and his taste vegetarian)
and his lack of sleep (he stayed awake at night in order to write).
He himself tended to believe that he was fated to stand apart
from normal life and thus go against the rules of healthy living.
Throughout the long correspondence with Felice which began in
September 1912 Kafka thought that he was probably doomed
never to achieve a lasting and fulfilling relationship with her or
with any other person. He made such a relationship with her all
the more impossible by insisting that it must be based on a
complete understanding and therefore on a completely honest
avowal of the exaggeratedly impossible person he was in his own
eyes. When no letter from her arrived he imagined that he must
have alienated and lost her. That might be no great loss perhaps
if his marriage to literature, as he later called it, proved fruitful,
but a terrible loss if, as he constantly feared, he would never
achieve much as a writer. On 15th and 16th November he
received no letter from Felice. He began writing *Die
Verwandlung* on the 17th. On the 14th he had written to say that
he could never marry and have children and that it might be
better if their correspondence ceased. Thus he had reason to
suspect that she might want to have no more to do with him, and
to see himself as an utterly worthless person, even though her
letter delivered on the 17th explained her silence as the result of
illness. On the 18th he wrote to her that he was working on his
story:

mit einem unbegrenzten Verlangen, mich in sie auszu-
gießen, deutlich von aller Trostlosigkeit aufgestachelt. Von
so vielem bedrängt, über Dich in Ungewissem, gänzlich
unfähig, mit dem Bureau auszukommen ... (BrF., p.105)

The office work was now not so much a duty owed to his parents
as a hateful burden, meaningful and necessary only if it were to
provide the financial basis for marriage to Felice. In his despair
over her he probably imagined, not for the first time, refusing to
go to work. There is, however, in *Die Verwandlung* no mention
of a girlfriend. Her place is taken by Gregor's sister Grete. For
on 7 November 1912 Kafka's youngest and favourite sister Ottla
had turned against him and sided with his parents. The rift with
Ottla was soon healed, but that night Kafka entertained
thoughts of suicide.

In 1911 Kafka had joined with his eldest sister's husband, Karl
Hermann, in founding an asbestos factory. He was the sleeping
partner in this business which began with twenty-five employees.
But he borrowed from his father to provide his capital invest-
ment (that this debt weighed on him like guilt may account for
the significance of the double meaning of 'Schuld' in *Die
Verwandlung*). Already in March 1912 he was so worried about
the economic viability of the venture and the obvious failure of
his desperate attempt to live up to the image of a middle-class
entrepreneur that he contemplated suicide. In November his
whole family insisted that he spend his afternoons in the factory
(his office work finished at 2 or 2.30 p.m. since he took no lunch
break). That meant no afternoon exercise and rest in
preparation for writing late into the night, or no possiblity of
writing. Kafka believed that he had no understanding of
business matters so that the sacrifice of his time and energy
would be wasted anyway. Only the intervention of Max Brod
who saw the real danger of suicide changed the minds of Kafka's
parents. But most hurtful of all Ottla, who usually took her
brother's part and understood his urge to write, agreed that he
must devote himself to the factory. This 'betrayal' by Ottla
becomes in the story the transformation of Grete from friend
into foe. Since Felice would surely also not tolerate relations

with an 'Ungeziefer' for long, a similar development in her was to be feared, and the sister in *Die Verwandlung* comes to play a part even more decisive than that of the father.

The sixty-year old Hermann Kafka had not retired from business after bankruptcy. But his business did not do well in 1912 and the weddings of his daughters were a drain on his resources. Bankruptcy was not inconceivable. His health was a matter of concern (though like Herr Samsa he might well be tougher than he seemed or pretended). He might not work much longer, in which case Kafka himself would have to support parents and Ottla. *Die Verwandlung* embodies the worst of Kafka's fears at this time: obliged to support his family he is incapable of doing so and is therefore rejected by them; that rejection mirrors Kafka's own view of himself and attitudes in society in general; he has no chance of marriage and no literary vocation to give meaning to his life. The story is set in a flat that the Samsas have occupied for five years very like the apartment at Niklasstraße 36 occupied by the Kafka family since June 1907. The view from the windows is quite different, but Kafka's room there, like Gregor's, lay between living-room and his parents' room and was connected by doors with both and with the hall. On occasions it was used to store unwanted objects, a circumstance that is exaggerated in the third part of the story. The noisy charwoman is loosely based on a housekeeper employed by the Kafkas. Gregor's sleeplessness and lack of appetite after his metamorphosis and his vegetarian tastes before it have their basis in Kafka's biography. But in November 1912 Ottla was twenty, Felice twenty-five, while Grete is only seventeen. The lodgers in the story are invented. The Jewish dimension of Kafka's problems may have seemed less significant to him in 1912 than the burning question of his relationship to his family, for the Samsas in the story are Catholics. Kafka selects, exaggerates and transforms reality in the process of writing. *Die Verwandlung* starts from Kafka's subjectively distorted experiences of November 1912 and a caricature of his wretched self; it is an exercise in self-torture and self-parody. Fear and desire are inextricably linked in this story; for the fear of rejection contains a wish to escape commitment. Such a para-

doxical attitude is expressed in the *Brief an den Vater* where
Kafka writes of the imagined loss of an Ottla who has gone over
to their father, and yet of the joy of contemplating the unity of
father and daughter and the former's happiness in particular
(H., p.141).

Because Kafka felt insecure as a person and was conscious of
this instability, he noticed how almost involuntarily he would
adapt himself to please others and even ape others. In a diary
entry dated 30th September 1911 he noted that this talent for
'metamorphosing' himself was as if dictated by an alien force
within him. Even if they could be seen as an act of volition, such
transformations bore witness to a division of the self. In the
early story *Hochzeitsvorbereitungen auf dem Lande*, which
dates from 1907, the hero Raban dreams of avoiding a meeting
with his fiancée (and the acceptance of social responsibility) by
dividing himself into two: his clothed body will fulfil the
burdensome obligation, but his true self will remain in bed, in
peace:

> 'Ich habe, wie ich im Bett liege, die Gestalt eines großen
> Käfers, eines Hirschkäfers oder eines Maikäfers, glaube
> ich ... Eines Käfers große Gestalt, ja.' (H., p.10)

Tired of work, of his fellow men, and of the workings of his own
mind, Raban imagines his transformation into a splendid insect.
The germ of Samsa's metamorphosis may be found here,
although between 1907 and 1912 the dream has become a nightmarish reality, escape has become guilt, the splendid beetle a
filthy vermin. But already in 1907 Kafka complained of leading
an inhuman existence ('da ich so viehisch lebe' (Br., p.51)), and
in 1908 of being hunted like a wild animal in the office (Br.,
p.55). In sketches written in his diary in the summer of 1910 a
bachelor figure moans that he has little strength and can only
crawl, 'nicht besser als ein Ungeziefer'; of the same man it is said
that he can only live as a hermit or a parasite. Lack of the
strength needed to play a responsible role in society, at work, or
as husband and parent, of the strength to fight life's battles, had
become associated with the image of an insect. A letter of 1st

November 1912 adds a further image which is taken into the
story: when Kafka did not have the strength to write, 'dann lag
ich auch schon auf dem Boden, wert hinausgekehrt zu werden'
(BrF., p.65).

Kafka's vivid imagination was fed by his self-deprecation
which itself was encouraged by the deprecation of his father who
did not shrink from colourful language. Regarding a Yiddish
actor whom Kafka befriended as a social pariah, he described
him to Kafka as vermin and a dog infested with fleas. Kafka
recorded this outburst as a judgment on himself.

Kafka naturally thought in images. An example from a letter
to a friend written in 1903 illustrates this habit. It also throws
some light on the significance of the window in *Die
Verwandlung* as an opening on the outside world not unrelated
to communication with people:

> Unter allen den jungen Leuten habe ich eigentlich nur mit
> Dir gesprochen ... Du warst, neben vielem andern, auch
> etwas wie ein Fenster für mich, durch das ich auf die
> Gassen sehen konnte. Allein konnte ich das nicht, denn
> trotz meiner Länge reiche ich noch nicht bis zum Fenster-
> brett. (Br., p.20)

Writing to the same friend in 1904, Kafka describes an inner
experience and begins to develop an image into a story; he
speaks of attempting to read and digest the almost two thousand
pages of Hebbel's diaries:

> ganz spielerisch anfangs, bis mir aber endlich so zu Mute
> wurde wie einem Höhlenmenschen, der zuerst im Scherz
> und in langer Weile einen Block vor den Eingang seiner
> Höhle wälzt, dann aber, als der Block die Höhle dunkel
> macht und von der Luft absperrt, dumpf erschrickt und
> mit merkwürdigem Eifer den Stein wegzuschieben sucht.
> Der aber ist jetzt zehnmal schwerer geworden und der
> Mensch muß in Angst alle Kräfte spannen, ehe wieder
> Licht und Luft kommt. (Br., p.27)

In his feeling of unworthiness Kafka compares himself with animals, in his utter lack of energy with inanimate or dying things:

> kraftlos wie das Blatt im Herbstwind sich von seinem
> Baume entfernt und überdies: ich war niemals an diesem
> Baume, im Herbstwind ein Blatt, aber von keinem Baum.
> (H., p.176)

In this one sentence a simile becomes a metaphor, and an image taken from reality becomes the basis of an image of a physical impossibility: only the notion of a dead leaf tossed by the wind, a leaf that never drew nourishment from a tree nor had any stable hold on life, seems adequate to convey the writer's condition, which is one of exclusion from the normal conditions of nature and life.

Kafka's emotional and mental responses to his own experience account for *Die Verwandlung* both in broad outline and in much detail. It is likely that his imagination was also shaped by books that he had read. Fairy stories may have played their part, and Ovid's *Metamorphoses*, and *The Double* by Dostoyevsky, which like *Die Verwandlung* opens with the hero waking to find himself in a strange state that cannot be dismissed as a dream. Indeed the possible literary influences on *Die Verwandlung* are many.

By exploring and giving literary shape to his fears Kafka hoped, as he informed Felice while he was writing *Die Verwandlung*, to liberate and cleanse himself from them:

> Was ist das doch für eine ausnehmend ekelhafte
> Geschichte ... ekelhaft ist sie grenzenlos und solche Dinge,
> siehst Du, kommen aus dem gleichen Herzen, in dem Du
> wohnst und das Du als Wohnung duldest. Sei darüber
> nicht traurig, denn, wer weiß, je mehr ich schreibe und je
> mehr ich mich befreie, desto reiner und würdiger werde ich
> vielleicht für Dich, aber sicher ist noch vieles aus mir
> hinauszuwerfen und die Nächte können gar nicht lang
> genug sein für dieses übrigens äußerst wollüstige Geschäft.
> (BrF., p.117)

Kafka did not free himself from the insecurity and guilt which in *Die Verwandlung* reveals itself as aggression and withdrawal. His later dismissive remarks on the story and on its ending in particular were no doubt motivated be feelings that had as much to do with the real people (including himself) who are distorted in it as with any purely aesthetic concerns. If he wrote of Gregor Samsa in the third person it was because there were, as he allows Raban of *Hochzeitsvorbereitungen auf dem Lande* to recognise, certain truths about himself that could be expressed only under the pretence that they did not apply specifically to him:

> 'Und solange du *man* sagst an Stelle von *ich*, ist es nichts und man kann diese Geschichte aufsagen, sobald du aber dir eingestehst, daß du selbst es bist, dann wirst du förmlich durchbohrt und bist entsetzt.' (H., p.8)

(Perhaps this quotation helps to explain why he occasionally lapses from 'er' into 'man' in *Die Verwandlung*.) But the pretence of *Die Verwandlung*, the exaggeration, the play of the imagination, while allowing Kafka to distance himself from his problems, also enmeshed him in them. There was some consolation to be found in transforming uncontrollable situations and fancies into a carefully measured utterance. Yet the control was largely illusory: an instinctive urge was in operation. It was an urge not simply to confess guilt, but also to demand understanding, to attack those who condemned him, and to prove his worth as a creative writer. The story even contained an implied attack on Felice whose rejection of him was perhaps the more terrible because it was as yet a possibility rather than a fact. By removing a serious personal problem from the sphere of reality and rational control, by exaggerating it to an extent that was objectively ridiculous, the story did not facilitate a real solution to that problem. It was in Janury 1914 when Kafka had just proposed marriage to Felice, when he therefore envisaged a real solution and hoped that he was not after all condemned to failure as a human being and an object of revulsion to all normal and nice people, that he wrote in his diary:

Großer Widerwille vor 'Verwandlung'. Unlesbares Ende.
Unvollkommen bis in den Grund.

5. More Perspectives

On completing *Das Urteil* Kafka noted in his diary on 23rd September 1912 that his thoughts naturally turned to Sigmund Freud. The father of psychoanalysis, whose theories of the unconscious and on the importance of sexuality and childhood experience for the functioning of the individual psyche shocked and excited Kafka's contemporaries, appeared, most especially in his investigations into a son's resentment of his father, to offer insight into such a story and a mind like Kafka's. Kafka observed in 1917 (Br., p.169) that Freudian theories could be crudely abused and debased. He was no Freudian. Nevertheless he believed that his strained relations with his father were central to his own life and his writing. On 11th February 1913 he recorded in his diary that he was not fully aware of the meanings implicit in *Das Urteil*, as if in that story he had mobilised energies beyond his conscious control; going at least half-way along the path of Freudian analysis, he recognised that his own name and Felice Bauer's were encoded in the tale and that one of its characters represented a force within the psyche of its hero:

> Anläßlich der Korrektur des 'Urteil' schreibe ich alle Beziehungen auf, die mir in der Geschichte klargeworden sind, soweit ich sie gegenwärtig habe. Es ist dies notwendig, denn die Geschichte ist wie eine regelrechte Geburt mit Schmutz und Schleim bedeckt aus mir herausgekommen ... Der Freund ist die Verbindung zwischen Vater und Sohn, er ist ihre größte Gemeinsamkeit ... Das Gemeinsame ist alles um den Vater aufgetürmt, Georg fühlt es nur als Fremdes, Selbständig-Gewordenes ...

There is no such commentary by Kafka on *Die Verwandlung*. But it too, because it is like a dream, seems particularly suited to the application of psychoanalysis which assumes that in imaginative fiction, as in dreams, depths of the personality usually repressed emerge, though largely in disguised form; the analyst can penetrate this disguise and pin-point the correlation between the author's neurosis and his dream-fiction. Though at least one commentator[7] has seen *Die Verwandlung* as a consciously sceptical response to Freud's early work, it is not usually assumed that Kafka knowingly exploited the ideas of Freud nor that his knowledge of them is relevant to the analyst's task. Rather the analyst may use any theory, whether Freudian or not, that he holds to be valid. Among interpreters of psycho-analytic bent there is considerable unanimity of basic diagnosis: *Die Verwandlung* betrays an Oedipus complex, hatred of the father, fear of him, and guilt. Orthodox Freudians argue that its causes lie in Kafka's childhood and that his resentment of his father was fundamentally a case of sexual rivalry centred on the mother. They are not surprised that Kafka was unaware of the sexual significance of his boyhood experiences, nor that the mother-fixation becomes in the story an incestuous desire for the sister, for they make allowance for the cunning that represses the truth of the unconscious. Gregor's regression into boyhood or infancy fits into this interpretation: it is held to be typical of neurotics, and the Oedipus complex to be characteristic of an early stage in the development of the male child. Less plausible is the assertion that Gregor suffers from a castration complex; to achieve this reading the critic needs to place faith in the Freudian hypothesis of fixed symbols according to which, for instance, round objects such as apples have an indisputably sexual significance. Attempts to prove that Gregor, revelling in filth, has regressed to the supposed anal phase of a child's development also appear forced.

The Oedipus complex as an explanation for Kafka's story can be neither proved nor disproved. It is one way of justifying the impression that *Die Verwandlung* treats a case of psychopathology. Those who are sceptical of the Freudian emphasis on sexuality and reliance on the murky unconscious may prefer, in the spirit of Freud's junior colleague, Alfred Adler, to interpret

[7] H. Binder, *Motiv und Gestaltung bei Franz Kafka* (Bonn, Bouvier, 1966), pp.98, 368ff.

the Oedipus complex as a more conscious battle for superiority, a failure to adjust to the demands of maturity; and to see in Gregor a maladjusted attempt to overcome feelings of inferiority by setting himself an impossible goal and using illness as an excuse for his inability to attain it. The inferiority complex then becomes the cause of Gregor's metamorphosis or of that aversion to his own body which some have believed that it signals. Or one can note in Gregor an inability either to assert his own individuality or to identify with the attitudes and demands of others; such fear of both autonomy and dependence is according to another Freudian schismatic, Otto Rank, symptomatic of the neurotic.

The application of different psychoanalytical theories to *Die Verwandlung* can lead to many differing conclusions. Freud's theories themselves allow for various interpretations. It is possible to apply to the story, instead of or in addition to his ideas on the id, the ego and the superego, his hypothesis that there is in the psychic activity of every person a conflict between a life instinct and a death instinct. Depending on which techniques of disguising the unconscious truth are thought to operate in the narrative, Gregor may be said to project his own aggression on to his father, or to absorb, through an operation called introjection, parental demands and the attitudes of society into his own conscience. It can be argued that Gregor's guilt is both self-imposed and forced upon him by others, the metamorphosis a representation of a wish to escape responsibility, of sadistic aggressiveness, and of a masochistic urge to self-punishment. Freud recognised such complications in mental events which were 'overdetermined', that is the result of several factors. To admit, as he did, cultural and historical influences on the individual's conscience is to allow the relevance of factors like Kafka's position as a partially assimilated Jew in the Prague of his time. Here psychoanalysis and social history begin to overlap as potential keys to Kafka's story. Some commentators go further and, on the basis of Jung's notion of archetypes and the collective unconscious, submit that behind the particular father lies the archetypal father God, and that reference to all Jewish history and myth, even to the history and myth of all

mankind, is permissible, indeed necessary, and enlightening.
The Jungian approach encourages a search for meanings con-
cerning divine judgment and the hope of salvation: it is one road
that leads to the religious approach to Kafka's work.

It is tempting to seize the lure of total comprehension which
many psychoanalytical interpretations of *Die Verwandlung*
purport to offer. But the most persuasive are those which do not
claim to exclude other readings, and which, in consequence,
recognise the labyrinthine quality of Kafka's story. It seems to
require for its explanation information that it does not contain,
and we may posit in the creative writer the ability darkly to fore-
see discoveries more systematically formulated by others. Yet it
is debatable whether psychoanalytical methods offer greater
insight into the story than empirical psychology which acknow-
ledges that Kafka's fiction reproduces emotional troubles of
which he was aware.

The sociological approach to *Die Verwandlung* also assumes
that the case of Gregor Samsa has general relevance, but puts its
emphasis on the mentality of the family, an authoritarian
society, and work which is a negation of freedom and therefore
of true humanity. Gregor's reaction to his job is taken to be
crucial and his father to represent an unjust society. He has
imposed on Gregor work that is uncongenial to him, humiliates
him and robs him of freedom. Gregor becomes a slave to the
clock. As his mother's complaint, 'Der Junge hat ja nichts im
Kopf als das Geschäft' (p.26), indicates, he is monopolised by
his job. His metamorphosis is an attempt to escape this slavery
and to vent his hatred of his masters. But his insect form also
manifests his bondage to a social order which demands the
tribute of conformity, stultifies the individual as a human being
and condemns individuality as a monstrosity. As a cog within an
economic machine Gregor cannot develop his proper potential
and is thus estranged from his true self and his humanity. He is
regarded by his family primarily as a provider of money rather
than as son and brother. He can neither fully accept as a duty the
role placed on him nor totally reject it. Such a reading of the
story may be further systematised by reference to Marx's

description of capitalism and his theory of alienation.[8] Though Gregor's father is not a grand capitalist he has exploited his son's labour to make a small 'Kapital' (p.43). Gregor has kept for his own use only a small part of his earnings, the 'surplus value' is appropriated by his father. The fruit of Gregor's work is not his own, he is therefore alienated from it and the work itself. Satisfying creative work, freely chosen, is not possible for the worker under capitalism. Gregor may be said to be reduced in his job to the status of an animal that exerts itself only to satisfy physical needs. Only at home and in his leisure time, says Marx, is the worker free, yet there he is inactive, just eats, drinks, copulates and sleeps; there too he is like an animal, alienated from proper human existence. This false freedom is seen in Gregor's aimless crawling over walls and ceiling. Both by the standards of true humanity and by the inhuman standards of his family he is a failure. He is the victim of inhuman attitudes and institutions. Some critics assert that Kafka gives an acute analysis of a social evil. But others (Marxists who demand a positive message in literature) criticise Kafka on the grounds that he fails to see the solution to the contradictions inherent in capitalism; they tend to view Gregor as a victim of his own blindness to the causes of his degradation. Others again warn that a story that reflects the dubious awareness of its hero cannot provide a critique of society.

Yet other commentators fasten on what they believe to be a positive characteristic of the insect Gregor, namely a rejection of materialism and a discovery of his true self. Paradoxically, they argue, it is in the monster that a proper regard for spiritual values is glimpsed. It happens above all when he senses the 'unbekannte Nahrung' promised by his sister's violin-playing (p.63). Reference to the significance of music in much German literature and in other works by Kafka is made to support this interpretation. In death, which brings a moment of charitable love, Gregor finds release from the material world. He achieves a higher awareness and self-knowledge, the realisation that there can be no salvation from the world in the world. The metamorphosis represents a metaphysical urge which is a longing for

[8] See *34*.

death. Many critics, again calling on evidence beyond the story itself, have identified the effect of the violin music with a vision of art or literature as a potential redemptive power. Though Gregor does not write, his wound and his longing for unknown nourishment can be linked with the same motifs elsewhere in Kafka to show that his is the fate of an artist figure. The story thus treats of a conflict between matter and spirit which transcends any particular age or form of society. Within the same interpretative framework it can, however, be maintained that the spiritual realm is only imagined and that the story contrasts the strength of pure vitality with the weakness of an existence anchored in spirituality; or that Gregor's reaction to the spiritual realm is impure, he fails to rise above the material world just as he fails to gain a firm hold on its physical reality.

Another shift of emphasis transforms this concern with spiritual values into a religious quest or mission. But once more those who agree that religious redemption is a major theme in *Die Verwandlung* arrive at contradictory conclusions: Gregor is a Messiah figure (or a false Messiah), like Christ he takes the guilt of others upon himself but is rejected by them — here we are asked to conjure with one debt to make it the sin of all and to juggle with the significance of Christmas, the third hour and an allusion to the apples in the Garden of Eden; Gregor has a remote glimpse of grace, his is the experience of man as a stricken creature which opens the gateway to the absolute; his condemnation by his father is a divine judgment, perhaps on a man who has not found the right relation between body and soul; God is notable by his absence rather than through his symbolic presence in the father; Gregor's sense of guilt is the anxiety which Kierkegaard believed to be the fundamental religious experience of the unbridgeable gulf between human ignorance and the will of God. Various traditions, both Jewish and Christian, are called on to decipher Kafka's text, as well as reference to the apparent omniscience of the father in *Das Urteil* and to the religious motifs in Kafka's other writings; but some think that Gregor denies the world and finds salvation, others that his death is degradation.

Interpretations that may be included under the headings of the sociological and religious approaches are largely speculative, their treatment of details in the text debatable and often unconvincing. But in principle they are not divorced from issues that concerned the author and may be reflected, however dimly, in *Die Verwandlung*. Like theories on the workings of the human psyche, questions of the social basis of injustice and misery and of the existence of spiritual truths and their relevance to the contemporary world occupied thinking men at a time when faith in science and technology, positivism and materialism seemed ripe for revision, yet conventional idealistic and religious beliefs lacked the power to convince the majority. Kafka was interested in socialism. In his job he saw how an authoritarian system cowed the ordinary man, how terrible were working conditions in some factories, and at his brother-in-law's asbestos factory he observed that the women workers while at work were somehow unfeminine and non-human. As a schoolboy he was a determined atheist, but before 1912 he had begun to show interest in the religious traditions of his people and especially in the Hasidic faith of those Jews of Eastern Europe who, he felt, had much to teach a Western Jew like himself. If he felt excluded from belief, he tended to interpret this as exclusion not just from knowledge of God's will, but also from a proper relationship with reality, the world of the senses and fellow human beings. In his diary of 21st August 1913 he noted his affinity with the mind of Kierkegaard, and on 24th November 1911, 'Auch im Talmud heißt es: Ein Mann ist ohne Weib kein Mensch'. Perhaps the very absence of piety in the Samsa family reflects Kafka's belief that his generation had been cut off from their religious and racial roots by the actions of their fathers.

The suspicion, often the conviction, that man's thinking had lost touch with the reality of existence was characteristic of the age in which Kafka lived. Optimistic forecasts, so typical of the previous decades, of progress through scientific understanding and technological control of nature seemed to be belied by an increase in social problems and individual misery. It was a time of doubts about man's ability to comprehend the world and about the rationality of existence itself. Metaphysical pessimism was rife. So too were various forms of mysticism, especially those which attempted to bring together both modern scientific and ancient intuitive thinking. Recent advances in knowledge, Freud, quantum physics, Einstein's theory of relativity, persuaded many that reality was more mysterious than the previous generation had thought. Many, in the wake of the extraordinarily influential philosophy of Nietzsche, believed that life had its own principles which had little to do with reason and justice, conventional morality and Judaic-Christian spirituality, and more with physical strength, cunning, and the will to dominate and survive. Those ideas were not without influence on Kafka. He longed to lead a more natural form of existence and respected in others the health and strength he felt he lacked. He was attracted by Rudolf Steiner's anthroposophy and prepared to listen to and observe Jewish mystics and rabbis for whom miraculous powers were claimed. He was confused, and to a degree amused, by the variety of man's pretences to understand himself and the universe and to hold the key to his own redemption. We may certainly suppose that *Die Verwandlung* mirrors a profound uncertainty about the meaning of life, that it does not deny the possibility of spiritual truths, yet expresses awe, and suspicion, of an incomprehensible 'life-force' which many of his contemporaries posited and from which its hero is unaccountably estranged.

Much of modern philosophy attempts to describe or explain a gulf between man and essential reality, between thinking and being, and offers concepts which may be used in the search for universal meanings in *Die Verwandlung*. Schopenhauer's notion of man's enslavement to a blind will that brings him ceaseless suffering which is relieved temporarily by art, particularly music, is often invoked as an influence on and key to the story. So too are Nietzsche's ambivalent ideas on art and its relation to truth and human suffering. Bergson's distinction between clock time and experienced time, part of his rejection of the mechanistic world of science as a (convenient) fiction, is evidently applicable to the story. Potentially useful also, if one is seeking enlightenment from affinities rather than probable influences, are many aspects of twentieth-century thought. Alongside Barth's Protestant theology of crisis, another offshoot of Kierkegaardian thinking, Heidegger's analysis of conscious man's essential difference from the world of things and of the anguished choice necessary for authentic living, can be brought to bear on Kafka's tale. Sartre's concepts of anguish, disgust, the experience of the nothingness or negativity of human existence, and his idea of 'mauvaise foi', can serve a similar purpose, though Kafka's critics who refer to the existentialism of Sartre or Camus usually assume that Kafka describes a totally absurd world. But against those who hold that Kafka believes with them that human consciousness can overcome its own problems there are those who claim him as an ally in the battle against the self-consciousness which, they assert, kills Gregor Samsa. The question whether Kafka glorified unquestioning obedience to authority or independence and individuality is still a burning one in some quarters.

The majority of critics, by discovering in Kafka an attitude with which they can identify, justify their admiration for his work and satisfy their urge to understand and judge. That same urge motivates those others who condemn his work as a falsification of reality. But the multiplicity of responses to *Die Verwandlung* indicates that the story does not allow certain judgment. Like the *Brief an den Vater* it may imply that father and son are both quite blameless, helpless victims of character and circumstance, while admitting that this may be wishful thinking and a cowardly avoidance of moral issues. The problems facing the interpreter of *Die Verwandlung* are those that confront anyone seeking to explain human affairs: he may reduce them to a pattern of his own choosing but in the knowledge that other patterns and perspectives are possible, and that the key chosen is not necessarily dictated by or even appropriate to the matter before him in all its complexity. Kafka's story beings home to us the unsettling realisation that in trying to make sense of fiction or reality we must make assumptions about what is relevant and what we expect to find. It forces us to ask whether an apparently fantastic perspective may not uncover a hidden truth.

In *Die Verwandlung* Kafka questions the writer's claim to make sense of experience. He asks if the interpreter of life does not transform it beyond recognition. Is this transformation creative or destructive, does it seize the essential or grotesquely distort the living truth? Is the observer of reality necessarily removed from the experience of reality? Does he stand superior to it or is he utterly and parasitically dependent on it? The story may be seen to reflect the process of writing fiction and the workings of the interpretative intelligence. It is the analogy between the two operations which makes Kafka's and other writers' worries about the justification of fiction relevant to the concerns of the ordinary reader.

If the story must by its very nature as imaginative fiction transform any experience or set of ideas which constituted its material, then that must throw doubt on any attempt to explain it too simplistically through its dependence on the author's life and reading. The raw material of fiction becomes something different when placed in its fictional context, within a different pattern of relations. The methods used to comprehend real life may not be appropriate for the comprehension of art.

As Kafka questions, by implication in *Die Verwandlung* and explicitly elsewhere, the relation of fiction to reality and of thought to experience, so too he was concerned about the relationship of words to both thought and experience. Did not all words operate like metaphors as soon as they were used to point to feelings, abstract thoughts, relations? Kafka wrote:

> Die Sprache kann für alles außerhalb der sinnlichen Welt nur andeutungsweise, aber niemals auch nur annähernd vergleichsweise gebraucht werden, da sie, entsprechend der sinnlichen Welt, nur vom Besitz und seinen Beziehungen handelt. (H., p.68)

His parable on parables and the metaphoric use of language concludes that they can say only what was was known already, namely that the incomprehensible is incomprehensible (B., p.95). He felt the gap between words and what they were meant to describe. So *Die Verwandlung* may be seen in the light of modern linguistics as an investigation of the function of metaphor and of poetic utterance, indeed of language itself as a

means of communication and interpretation; of what happens
when we assume, as we invariably do, that signifier and signified
(in this case the man and the 'Ungeziefer' of Kafka's basic metaphor) are one and the same: the result is an absurdity, a dis-
tortion of the truth. Can one hope that this 'misuse' of language
may be creative and revealing? Again we need to look beyond
the seductively scientific terminology of modern linguistic
theory and to recognise that here is but another perspective from
which to view the ambiguity of the story and its challenge to
interpretation.

Do all the readings of *Die Verwandlung*, in total far too
numerous and varied[9] to be mentioned here, lead to one
conclusion? Surely they together point to the need to think carefully about the status of fiction and about the methodology of
literary interpretation. Where so many solutions to the same
problem are offered, none can be entirely convincing, for each
must leave something unsaid even if it does not twist or invent
evidence. Do we not feel that the interpretations somehow fail to
grasp the reality of the tale? But surely also they together point
to the richness of a story which reflects so many facets of
modern thought and sensibility, or to its magical ability to meta-
morphose itself according to the expectations of the observer.
Perhaps, too, the perplexity of its commentators shows that the
story is like life as Kafka described it in his *Brief an den Vater*: it
is not a puzzle whose pieces can, with patience and skill, be fitted
together to form a predetermined, regular shape:

> So können natürlich die Dinge in Wirklichkeit nicht
> aneinanderpassen, wie die Beweise in meinem Brief, das
> Leben ist mehr als ein Geduldspiel (H., p.162)

To read *Die Verwandlung* is to be exposed to a vivid experience
which survives all attempts to explain it and never ceases to pro-
voke wonder and reflection.

---

[9] 6 and 7 list the literature according to the several fashions or approaches and
emphases.

Select Bibliography

WORKS BY KAFKA

Stories by Kafka published in book form:

Betrachtung (Leipzig, Rowohlt, 1913)
Der Heizer: ein Fragment (Leipzig, Wolff, 1913)
Das Urteil: eine Geschichte (Leipzig, Wolff, 1916)
Die Verwandlung (Leipzig, Wolff, 1916)
In der Strafkolonie (Leipzig, Wolff, 1919)
Ein Landarzt: kleine Erzählungen (Leipzig and Munich, Wolff, 1919)
Ein Hungerkünstler: vier Geschichten (Berlin, Die Schmiede, 1924)

The collected works, ed. Max Brod (*Gesammelte Schriften*, 3rd edition, Frankfurt a.M., S. Fischer):

Der Prozeß (1950)
Das Schloß (1951)
Tagebücher 1910-1923 (1951)
Briefe an Milena, ed. W. Haas (1952)
Erzählungen (1952)
Amerika (1953)
Hochzeitsvorbereitungen auf dem Lande und andere Prosa aus dem Nachlaß (1953)
Beschreibung eines Kampfes: Novellen, Skizzen, Aphorismen aus dem Nachlaß (1954)
Briefe 1902-1924 (1958)
Briefe an Felice und andere Korrespondenz aus der Verlobungszeit, ed. E. Heller and J. Born (1967)
Briefe an Ottla und die Familie, ed. H. Binder and K. Wagenbach (1974)

The critical edition, in progress (*Schriften, Tagebücher, Briefe: Kritische Ausgabe*, ed. J. Born et al (Frankfurt a.M., S. Fischer):

Das Schloß, ed. M. Pasley (1982)
Der Verschollene (Amerika), ed. J. Schillemeit (1983)

A convenient collection:

Sämtliche Erzählungen, ed. P. Raabe (Frankfurt a.M., Fischer Bücherei, 1970)

BIOGRAPHY

1. Wagenbach, K., *Franz Kafka: eine Biographie seiner Jugend 1883-1912* (Berne, Francke, 1958)
2. ——, *Franz Kafka in Selbstzeugnissen und Bilddokumenten* (Hamburg, Rowohlt, 1964)
3. Politzer, H. (editor), *Das Kafka-Buch: eine innere Biographie in Selbstzeugnissen* (Frankfurt a.M., Fischer, 1973)
4. Binder, H. (editor), *Kafka-Handbuch in zwei Bänden*, Vol.1: *Der Mensch und seine Zeit* (Stuttgart, Alfred Kröner, 1979)

BIBLIOGRAPHIES

5. Reiss, H.S., 'Recent Kafka Criticism 1944-1955: a Survey', in *18*
6. Beicken, P., *Franz Kafka: eine kritische Einführung in die Forschung* (Frankfurt a.M., Athenäum Fischer Taschenbuch, 1974)
7. Dietz, L., *Franz Kafka* (Stuttgart, Metzler, 1975)
8. Flores, A., *A Kafka Bibliography 1908-1976* (New York, Gordian Press, 1976)
9. ——, 'Bibliographical Supplement' in *16*. See also *13*

STUDIES

10. Anders, G., *Franz Kafka* (London, Bowes and Bowes, 1960), first published as *Kafka: Pro und Contra* (Munich, C.H. Beck, 1951)
11. Beicken, P. (editor), *Erläuterungen und Dokumente: Franz Kafka, 'Die Verwandlung'* (Stuttgart, Reclam, 1983)
12. Binder, H., *Kafka-Kommentar zu sämtlichen Erzählungen* (Munich, Winkler, 1975)
13. Corngold, S., *The Commentators' Despair: the Interpretation of Kafka's 'Metamorphosis'* (Port Washington, N.Y., Kennikat Press, 1973), with critical bibliography
14. Flores, A. (editor), *The Kafka Problem* (New York, New Directions, 1946)
15. Flores, A., and H. Swander (editors), *Franz Kafka Today* (Madison, University of Wisconsin Press, 1958)
16. Flores, A. (editor), *The Kafka Debate* (New York, Gordian Press, 1977)
17. Foulkes, A.P., *The Reluctant Pessimist: a Study of Franz Kafka* (The Hague, Mouton, 1967)
18. Gray, R. (editor), *Kafka: a Collection of Critical Essays* (Englewood Cliffs, N.J., Prentice-Hall, 1962)
19. Gray, R., *Franz Kafka* (Cambridge, Cambridge University Press, 1973)
20. Heller, E., *Franz Kafka* (New York, Viking Press, 1975)
21. Heller, P., 'On not understanding Kafka' in *16*
22. Hibberd, J., *Kafka in Context* (London, Studio Vista, 1975)
23. Hutchinson, P., 'Red herrings or clues?' in *16*
24. Kuna, F., *Kafka: Literature as Corrective Punishment* (London, Paul Elek, 1974)

25.   —— (editor), *On Kafka: Semi-Centenary Perspectives* (London, Paul Elek, 1976)
26.   Landsberg, P., 'The Metamorphosis' in *14*
27.   Luke, F.D., 'The Metamorphosis' in *15*
28.   Pascal, R., *Kafka's Narrators: a Study of his Stories and Sketches* (Cambridge, Cambridge University Press, 1982)
29.   Pfeiffer, J., 'The Metamorphosis' in *18*
30.   Politzer, H., *Franz Kafka: Parable and Paradox* (Ithaca, N.Y., Cornell University Press, 1962)
31.   Rolleston, J., *Kafka's Narrative Theater* (University Park and London, Pennsylvania State University Press, 1974)
32.   Sokel, W., *Franz Kafka: Tragik und Ironie* (Munich and Vienna, Albert Langen — Georg Müller, 1964)
33.   ——, *Franz Kafka* (New York and London, Columbia University Press, 1966)
34.   ——, 'Von Marx zum Mythos: das Problem der Selbstentfremdung in Kafkas "Verwandlung"', *Monatshefte* 73 (1981), pp.6-22
35.   Stern, J.P. (editor), *The World of Franz Kafka* (London, Weidenfeld and Nicolson, 1980)
36.   Thorlby, A., *A Student's Guide to Kafka* (London, Heinemann, 1972)
37.   Wiese, B. v., *Die deutsche Novelle von Goethe bis Kafka*, Vol.2 (Düsseldorf, August Bagel, 1962), pp.319-45

Supplementary Bibliography

WORKS BY KAFKA

38. *Tagebücher (Schriften, Tagebücher, Briefe: Kritische Ausgabe)*, ed. H.-G. Koch et al. (Frankfurt a.M., S. Fischer, 1990)
39. *Die Verwandlung*, ed. P. Hutchinson and M. Minden (London, Methuen, 1985, reprinted London, Routledge, 1993, 1994). German text with good introduction and notes in English.

BIOGRAPHIES

40. Hayman, R., *Kafka: a Biography of Kafka* (London, Weidenfeld and Nicholson, 1981)
41. Pawel, E., *The Nightmare of Reason: a Life of Franz Kafka* (London, Harvill Press, 1984)

SECONDARY LITERATURE

42. Robertson, R., *Kafka: Judaism, Politics and Literature* (Oxford, Clarendon Press, 1985)